Peyote

Nancy Ross-Flanigan

— The Drug Library —

Enslow Publishers, Inc.

40 Industrial Road   PO Box 38
Box 398   Aldershot
Berkeley Heights, NJ 07922   Hants GU12 6BP
USA   UK

http://www.enslow.com

Paperback edition published in 2001.
First library edition published in 1997.

Library of Congress Cataloging-in-Publication Data

Ross-Flanigan, Nancy.
    Peyote / Nancy Ross-Flanigan.
        p. cm. — (The Drug Library)
    Includes bibliographical references and index.
    Summary: Discusses the history, use, and effects of peyote, as well
as the role of peyote in Native American religious rituals.
    ISBN 0-7660-1928-4 (pbk)
    ISBN 0-89490-851-0 (library ed.)
    1. Peyote—Juvenile literature. 2. Peyotism—Juvenile literature.
[1. Peyote. 2. Drug abuse. 3. Indians of North America—Religion.]
I. Title. II. Series.
RM666.P48R67 1997
615'.32356—DC21   96-40105
                                  CIP
                                   AC

Printed in the United States of America

10 9 8 7 6 5 4 3

Photo Credits: Audrey Jones, pp. 34, 53, 96; Dr. Stacy B. Schaefer, pp. 7, 15, 26,
30, 37, 65, 70; Nancy Ross-Flanigan, p. 86; Raymond Pokerwinski, pp. 59, 91;
Tom Mayers, p. 47.

Cover Photo: Dr. Stacy B. Schaefer.

Contents

Acknowledgments

I am greatly indebted to many people for their help and support. For providing information and photographs and for reviewing portions of the manuscript, I thank Nicholas Cozzi, Peter d'Errico, Rick Doblin, Jerry Frankenheim, Neal Goldsmith, Audrey Jones, Christopher Koenigsberg, Tom Mayers, Edward Pisachubbe, Stacy Schaefer, Richard Schwartz, Sylvia Thyssen, and Robert Billy Whitehorse. Fellow journalists Jim Jones, Jerry Kammer, and Ben Winton offered insights and access to sources. Most of all, I am grateful to Ray Pokerwinski for his good humor and loving support, and for installing a door on my office.

1

The History of Peyote

In a big circle, men and women sat listening to a musician and a song leader. Nearby a tray was filled with pieces of peyote and tea made from the plant. One at a time, the men and women got up and went to the center of the circle to dance and sing. Some danced around in a ring, others simply marked time with their feet. When they sang, their voices were flat and expressionless. From time to time they drank peyote tea. All night the singing and dancing went on. By dawn most of the people were so exhausted and intoxicated they could hardly move.[1]

This was the scene that Spanish missionary José Ortega described in 1690 after watching people of the Cora tribe in Western Mexico use peyote. Ortega, who called peyote a "diabolical root," was one of the first people to write about the peyote ritual.[2] However, peyote use began long before Ortega's account and continues today, mostly in Mexico and the southwestern United States.

No one knows who was first to use the small cactus called peyote. The top of a peyote cactus plant is known as a peyote button. Archeologists have found pieces of peyote in caves and rock shelters, where they believe it was used in ceremonies almost seven thousand years ago. Some experts think prehistoric people used it as long as ten thousand years ago.

Native Tribes and Peyote

Native tribes in Mexico and the United States have their own legends about how peyote was discovered. The Huichol people, for example, believe that some of their ancestors saw a deer one day. The deer took five steps and then disappeared. In the deer's tracks, peyote plants appeared. The Huichol tribe lives in a high desert region in Mexico. The people believe that corn, deer, and peyote are all forms of the same thing. All, they believe, are gifts from the gods. Every year Huichol people travel to a place called Wirikúta, where peyote grows. They believe that is where the first peyote was found in the deer's footprints.[3]

Peyote is an important part of their whole culture today, just as it has been for thousands of years. They use it as a painkiller, as a stimulant to make work easier, and as a spiritual tool in religious ceremonies. Some Huichol women take peyote during pregnancy and labor. They say it makes childbirth almost painless.[4] Although the Huichol people use peyote at celebrations, they say they do not use it just to get intoxicated. "Americans are looking for a Saturday night high," one Huichol man said. "Peyote is not like that."[5]

The Huichol people of Mexico have different words to describe peyote plants of different shapes.

Although not all Huichols use peyote, they all understand its influence on their culture. Anthropologist Stacy Schaefer, who has been visiting and studying the Huichol people for many years, says that peyote reinforces Huichol beliefs and strengthens family and community ties. It helps Huichol people understand themselves and the deeper meaning of life.[6] As one Huichol man explained to Schaefer, "peyote is everything, it is the crossing of the souls, it is everything that is." Without peyote, the man said, nothing else would exist.[7]

Peyote is so important that the Huichol people have many ways to describe it. They have different words for peyote plants of different shapes. Even Huichol art is influenced by peyote. Women weave and embroider cloth in patterns that resemble peyote plants. The weavers say the patterns come to them in peyote visions, and they believe it is their sacred duty to capture and share them. If they do not, bad things may happen to them, they believe.[8] Huichol artists also make colorful "paintings" of yarn pressed into beeswax, inspired by visions they have had while under the influence of peyote.

Another native Mexican tribe, the Tarahumara, has used peyote for centuries, mainly as medicine. The Tarahumara people drink powdered peyote in water for general health and long life. They also make a paste out of powdered peyote and use it to treat snake bites, burns, wounds, and arthritis. Taken in small amounts, peyote helps them ward off hunger, thirst, and fatigue while hunting.

Healing Powers

Whoever used peyote first probably used it because they believed it had healing powers. People who lived long ago looked at illness differently than doctors do today. They believed illness was caused by spirits working in the body. The only way to be cured was to communicate with the spirits. When they discovered plants, such as peyote, that had strange effects on their minds and bodies, they believed those effects helped connect them to the spirit world.[9]

The first written description of peyote's physical and psychological effects came from the Franciscan missionary Bernardo de Sahagún. "Those who eat or drink it see visions either frightful or laughable," he wrote in the mid-1500s. He added, "It stimulates them and gives them sufficient spirit to fight and have neither fear, thirst, nor hunger, and they say it guards them from all danger."[10]

Peyote and Christianity

Many of the Spanish explorers and missionaries who came to Mexico in the 1500s through the 1700s disapproved of the native people's peyote use. They considered it sinful, in the same category as murder and cannibalism.[11] One priest, Padre Andrés Pérez de Ribas, reported that peyote was connected with "heathen rituals and superstitions," and that native people used it to get in touch with evil spirits through "diabolic fantasies."[12] The Catholic Church, which was especially opposed to the use of peyote to foretell the future, banned its use and forgave the sins of anyone who had used it before the ban. People who used peyote after that were investigated and punished. Some were even tortured and killed. Still that did not stop its use.

Many native people simply combined their new Christian beliefs with their old beliefs about peyote. Some believed that a patron saint named El Santo Niño de Peyotl lived among peyote plants in the hills.[13]

Peyote Use in the United States

By the 1880s the practice of using peyote in ceremonies had spread to the United States. No one is sure how that happened, but the Lipan Apaches may have learned the ceremonies from native Mexicans. The Lipan Apaches taught it to the Kiowas and Comanches of Oklahoma, who in turn taught it to other Oklahoma Native Americans. From Oklahoma tribes, peyote use spread to other Plains tribes.

Around the time that peyote use began to spread, United States government policies were weakening Native American traditions. Forced from their homelands and made to live on reservations, Native Americans were searching for ways to keep their culture alive. Peyote ceremonies may have appealed to them as a means of reclaiming some of their old ways. Perhaps they also believed that peyote's strange effects would somehow bring them power and help them to solve their problems.[14]

Ironically, some of the policies and institutions that were designed to make Native Americans conform to white ways may have actually aided in the spread of peyote use. For example, Catholic missions were supposed to be places where priests converted Native Americans to Christianity. Yet the missions also served as gathering places where Native Americans could share their knowledge of peyote and even buy and sell the cactus. The establishment of reservations played a role, too. Before the United States government set up reservations, different tribes of Native Americans lived far apart. They did not come in contact with one another very often. But when many tribes were forced to move to reservations in what is now Oklahoma, there was much more opportunity for contact—and for learning from one another about peyote.

Schools set up strictly for Native Americans also may have contributed to the spread of peyote use. Native American children were sent to boarding schools, where they learned English, Christianity, and the customs of white society. The schools intended to "civilize" Native Americans and make them forget their own traditions. That was not always what happened, however. With a common language—English—young Native Americans could more easily exchange the traditions and lore of their own culture. It is not clear whether any young Native Americans learned about peyote while away at school, but many of them became peyotists (people who use peyote in ceremonies) when they returned to the reservations. The intertribal friendships they formed in school may have further paved the way for the spread of peyote use.

The Ghost Dance

One other important influence on the spread of peyote was something called the Ghost Dance. The Ghost Dance was a religion that attracted thousands of Native Americans in the 1890s. It combined traditional Native American dance ceremonies with Christian teachings. Native Americans who practiced the Ghost Dance believed that by living good lives, dancing regularly, working hard, and trying to get along with white people, they could reverse the changes that had made their lives so unhappy. Their dead relatives would come back to life, white people would disappear, and everything would be like the "good old days" again. The Ghost Dance religion did not involve peyote. It did, however, offer another way for Native Americans of different tribes to get to know one another and share traditions. Since many people practiced both the Ghost Dance and peyote religion, this sharing of traditions helped spread peyotism (the ceremonial use of peyote).[15]

Some Native American leaders opposed peyote use, but others became "peyote prophets." They conducted peyote ceremonies and taught others how to use it. Each peyote prophet had his own, slightly different, version of the peyote ceremony and his own loyal followers.

The Quanah Parker Way

One especially powerful peyote leader was Quanah Parker, who lived from 1845 to 1911. Parker was a respected Comanche chief who learned the peyote ceremony from two Lipan Apaches named Billy Chiwat and Pinero. For a while Chiwat and Pinero ran peyote meetings for Parker. Eventually, however, Parker began performing the ceremonies himself. He popularized the version known as the Half Moon Ceremony, named for the moon-shaped altar used in the ritual. The ceremony became so connected with Parker in people's minds, many called it the Quanah Parker Way.

Parker had been opposed to peyote when it first began to spread to Oklahoma. But something changed his mind. Nobody knows for sure what that was—there are different versions of the story. According to one version, Parker was gored by a bull while visiting his brother in Mexico. The wound was very serious, and he developed blood poisoning. Local Indians gave him a drink made from boiled green peyote, and he got well. Convinced that peyote had saved his life, he returned to Oklahoma and began spreading the word.

Parker, whose mother was white, was well liked by both Native Americans and whites. He never converted to Christianity, but he got along well with local missionaries and supported their efforts to educate Native American children in mission schools. Through his good relations with missionaries and Bureau of Indian Affairs officials, he was able to defend Native Americans' right to use peyote. His usual approach was to quietly and calmly try to convince people that peyote was not harmful. When that did not work, he would sometimes pretend to go along with those who opposed peyote. All the while, however, he still secretly promoted its use. For example, he once told the Bureau of Indian Affairs that his people would stop using peyote when their current supply ran out. Then he talked officials into letting him send two men to Mexico to bring back a little peyote, just to help longtime users taper off gradually. To the exasperation of Indian Affairs agents, Parker's representatives came back with a truck full of eight thousand peyote buttons.

When Parker fell ill and died, doctors said the cause was asthmatic arthritis. Parker and his family had other explanations. When Parker learned he was dying, he believed he was being punished for the sin of charging money to heal people with peyote. "I have made a great mistake to demand a fee for helping the meek and poor," he said just before he died. "For this I must pay the price by giving up my own life."[16]

Parker's daughter, who did not share her father's belief in the power of peyote, later testified at a congressional hearing on a bill to ban the drug. In her testimony she said it was her father's addiction to peyote that killed him.[17] There is no medical evidence that peyote is addictive, but in those days, some people thought that it was.

The Big Moon Ceremony

Another famous peyote leader who lived around the same time as Parker was John Wilson. Wilson was a Caddo medicine man who became a peyote "roadman" in 1880. Roadman is the term for a person who leads peyote ceremonies. Unlike Parker, Wilson was not a powerful chief, and he did not campaign for Native Americans' right to use peyote. He simply taught his version of the peyote ritual, called the Big Moon Ceremony, to many other people.

Wilson's Big Moon Ceremony was similar to the ceremony Quanah Parker had learned from the Lipan Apaches. Wilson claimed, however, that nobody taught him how to perform the peyote ritual. He said he learned it directly "from the peyote." One day in 1880 he and his wife packed up a wagon and drove to a secluded site by a creek. They camped there for about two weeks. During that time, Wilson took peyote frequently, eating about fifteen pieces each time. In his visions he saw symbols that represented events in the life of Christ. He also saw the "peyote road," a path leading from Christ's tomb to the moon. Peyote, which seemed to have a human form in Wilson's visions, gave him instructions. It told him to follow the peyote road for the rest of his life, increasing his knowledge step-by-step by continuing to use peyote. Peyote also told Wilson exactly how to conduct peyote rituals, how to sing peyote songs, and how to make all the

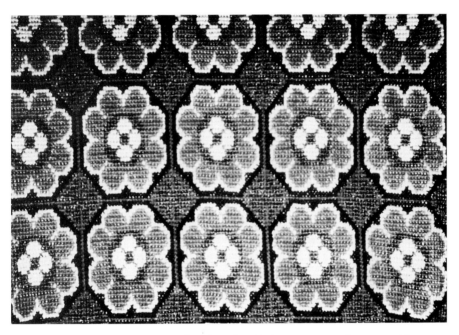

Huichol women weave and embroider cloth in patterns that resemble peyote plants.

sacred objects—the drum stick, feathered fan, gourd rattle, and prayer staff—to use in the ceremonies.[18]

Wilson's Big Moon Ceremony taught that peyote was a gift from God that could be used for healing, purifying the mind, and learning to tell good from evil. The Big Moon Ceremony used more Christian symbols and rituals than Parker's Half Moon Ceremony used.

As peyotism spread throughout Oklahoma and then to other states, the ceremonies became more church-like. Traditionally, peyote meetings were held in tipis, with earthen altars built inside and taken down after the meeting. The Osage started a new tradition of building eight-sided wooden peyote chapels with a concrete altar inside and a cross on the roof.

Eventually, the peyote religion became more organized. In 1914 peyotist Jonathan Koshiway started the Firstborn Church of Christ. It combined peyote ceremonies and Christianity in its worship services. The official documents of Koshiway's church did not mention peyote use. The Native American Church, organized just four years later, openly acknowledged its use of peyote. By 1920 the Native American Church had more than thirteen thousand members in thirty tribes.[19] Today, the church's two hundred fifty thousand members still use peyote ceremonially.[20] Members hold peyote ceremonies in tipis or peyote church buildings to give thanks; to celebrate births, holidays, and other happy events; to ask for guidance when going off to school or military service; and to be cured of diseases.

Just as native Mexican peyotists faced opposition from Spanish missionaries and rulers, Native American peyotists have had their opponents. Yet they also found support from some researchers and government officials.

Efforts to Ban Peyote Use

In the late 1800s and early 1900s some government officials and missionaries tried to get peyote banned because they thought it was a bad influence on Native Americans. Bureau of Indian Affairs agents sometimes paid white farmers to spy on peyote meetings and report who was there and what went on. In their reports to the Bureau of Indian Affairs, agents wrote that peyote sapped the physical strength and mental energy of Native Americans who used it. They claimed peyote ceremonies were just an excuse for getting high and said people had died from using the drug.

Missionaries also complained about peyote's effects on the people they were trying to convert. One wrote to the Bureau of Indian Affairs in 1903, saying that Saturday's all-night peyote ceremonies interfered with Sunday morning church services. The peyote ceremonies left participants "in such a state of stupefaction that it is utterly impossible to teach them anything from the word of God," he wrote. Peyote, he added, "is perhaps the chief hindrance to the efforts of the missionaries."[21]

Some of the negative opinions may have been shaped by the immoral behavior of a few peyote leaders. While men like Quanah Parker and John Wilson were well respected, others had bad reputations. Among the worst was Sam Lone Bear.

Lone Bear had toured the United States and Europe with Buffalo Bill Cody's Wild West Show. Later he traveled throughout the West, teaching peyotism. But Lone Bear was dishonest. He did magic tricks in peyote meetings, convincing people that the effects were caused by supernatural powers. He also sold cheap trinkets for high prices, claiming they had magic properties. He cheated people out of money and got in trouble with the law for kidnapping young girls. Eventually he was sent to prison. Native Americans who had been his followers later said that Lone Bear "used peyote bad" and "did not guide us in the right."[22]

Lone Bear's bad behavior led some Native Americans to lobby against peyotism. Gertrude Bonnin, a Dakota Sioux, was especially active. She successfully campaigned for laws prohibiting peyote use in Utah, North Dakota, South Dakota, and Colorado, and even attracted Denver society women to the cause. She also pressed for a federal ban on peyote.

While Bonnin actively campaigned against peyote, other Native Americans simply tried to ignore it. Peyotism never caught on among the Cherokee, Choctaw, Seminole, Creek, and Chickasaw. Christianity had been strong among these tribes for several generations, and many people felt loyal to the churches they had grown up in. These five tribes stressed education and middle-class values. Their members looked down on Native American traditions that they saw as primitive or heathen. To them, peyotism was an embarrassment and an evil influence.[23] Some people, however—both Native American and white—saw peyote as a good influence.

Jock Bull Bear had used peyote for thirty-two years. He explained in a 1918 *Washington Times* article how the drug had benefited him. He said he believed he had done well in life—raising six children, tending a small farm, and steering clear of alcohol and gambling—because of his peyote religion.

"Our religion, peyote members, as we might express it, are not against anything that is good," he wrote. "We are living uprightly under the United States flag, and helping to improve the condition of our Indian race, make them better Christians, and to live the real civilized life."[24]

18

Another Native American who never had used peyote testified before a congressional committee that he felt grateful to peyote for stopping "drunkenness and lawlessness" among his people. He also said that missionaries never had explained Christianity in a way Native Americans could understand. But peyote had helped them "think intelligently of God and of their relations to him."[25]

Between 1890 and 1918 James Mooney of the Smithsonian Institution's Bureau of American Ethnology lived for months at a time among Native Americans, mainly in Oklahoma. He sat in on peyote ceremonies and got to know many peyote leaders. He was so convinced of the benefits of peyote that he vigorously defended its use. A former newspaper reporter, he wrote many articles about peyote. He described the ceremonies in detail and explained the beliefs behind them. He even testified against a proposed bill to ban peyote. However, Mooney was criticized for standing up for peyote. The Bureau of Indian Affairs asked the Smithsonian to recall him, and he never was allowed to study peyotism in Oklahoma again.

Although the Bureau of Indian Affairs resented Mooney's interference, some Indian Affairs agents agreed with his opinions. One wrote:

> *In so far as I know the use of this drug has had no visible effect on its users most of them being just now in excellent health, nor has it had any bad effect on the social condition of those participating, for I am quite sure that the users of it will rank with the better class of our Indians.*[26]

Recreational Use of Peyote

For most of its long history, peyote has been used by native people for religious and health reasons. Yet there is another side to peyote. Since the late 1800s other people have experimented with peyote. At first serious researchers did most of the experiments. They were looking for ways to use peyote as medicine. However, some people used peyote out of curiosity. Some also tried mescaline, the main active ingredient found in peyote cactus. Mescaline is a chemical compound called an alkaloid. Along with several other alkaloids, mescaline gives peyote its mind-altering effect. When extracted from peyote and used by itself, mescaline produces effects similar to those of peyote. Fascinated by psychiatrists' theories on how mescaline affected the mind, the English writer Aldous Huxley volunteered to try it. He wrote about his experience in his 1954 book *The Doors of Perception*.

In the 1950s and 1960s the numbers of people using peyote and mescaline for inspiration or for kicks increased, as use of mind-altering drugs in general became more widespread. The poet Allen Ginsberg experimented with writing poetry under the influence of various drugs, including peyote. He wrote his long poem *Howl* after a night spent wandering the streets of San Francisco under the influence of peyote. Psychologist Timothy Leary, famous for experimenting with lysergic acid diethylamide (LSD), also experimented with mescaline. Twenty years after the famous rock concert Woodstock, guitarist Carlos Santana recalled that he was high on mescaline before he went on stage. He remembered praying, "Lord, help me to stay in tune and in time."[27]

Young people, too, tried peyote and mescaline. At one time students could buy mescaline in sandwich shops near the Harvard University campus. They could even order peyote through the mail. In 1960 a raid on the Dollar Sign Coffee House in New York's East Greenwich Village turned up 311 pieces of dried peyote.[28] Before the raid, coffee house customers could buy capsules filled with ground peyote over the counter.

Today peyote is most widely used by Native Americans in religious ceremonies. Many of peyote's effects may be unpleasant—nausea, vomiting, panic attacks, frightening visions, and feelings of being near death are not uncommon. Perhaps this is one reason why people who try it once for kicks are not likely to try it again.

Questions for Discussion

1. There have been many efforts to have the ceremonial use of peyote banned. Do you think the ceremonial use of peyote should have a place in Native American culture? Why? Why not?

2. If Native Americans are legally able to use peyote, should others have the same right? Why? Why not?

3. Do you think that using peyote for religious reasons is different than abusing other drugs for recreational reasons? Why? Why not?

2

The Peyote Plant

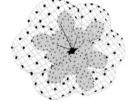

If you were hiking through the Texas desert near the Río Grande, you might step right over a peyote plant without even knowing it. The small, gray-green cactus hardly looks like anything worth noticing. It has no spines, branches or leaves, and it grows close to the ground. Underground is a long, carrot-shaped root. The only part you see above the ground is the plant's round, flat "head," shaped something like a turnip or a child's toy top. Each head is only about three inches across, but the plants sometimes form clusters of many heads—as big as six feet across.

In the center of each fleshy head is a fuzzy, round spot. If you happened to come across a peyote plant in early spring, you might see a short stalk coming out of the fuzzy spot, with a pinkish-white or pale yellow flower at the end. Later the flower matures into a club-shaped, pinkish-red fruit with wrinkly black seeds inside.

In hot, dry weather, the plant's head shrivels and shrinks into itself. It looks as if it is pulling its head into its neck. That may explain some folk legends about peyote. According to a Taos legend, a Native American man came across a peyote plant that was opening and closing.

> Then the plant told the Indian to come inside. But the opening was so small. Then it got bigger; it got to be a big hole in the ground, a square hole. The Indian went down the hole. There was a big hollow place down there in the ground, round like a kiva.[1]

A kiva is a round ceremonial building that is usually partly underground. The legend goes on to tell how the Native American man learned the peyote ritual from a man in the kiva.

Kiowa lore also mentions the mysterious shriveling peyote plant. As the Kiowa people say, "you must look closely at peyote, because it is like a mole when it comes on top of the ground—if you don't look closely it is gone again."[2]

A Scientific Description of Peyote

The first scientific description of the peyote plant came from Dr. Fernando Hernandez in 1628. Hernandez, the personal physician of King Philip II of Spain, was sent to the Americas to study Aztec medicine. Here is how he described the peyote plant:

> The root is of nearly medium size, sending forth no branches or leaves above the ground, but with a certain woolliness adhering to it on account of which it could not aptly be

*figured by me. Both men and women are said to be harmed
by it. It appears to be of a sweetish taste and moderately hot.
Ground up and applied to joints, it is said to give relief.
Wonderful properties are attributed to this root, if any faith
can be given to what is commonly said among them on this
point. It causes those devouring it to be able to foresee and
predict things . . .*[3]

Hernández also had an explanation for the peyote plant's odd
shrunken appearance. The plant "conceals itself in the ground, as if
it did not wish to harm those who discover it and eat it," he wrote.[4]

Early naturalists used various scientific names to describe
peyote. Peyote plants can look very different from one another,
so some naturalists who studied peyote specimens mistakenly
thought they were looking at many different species. There really
are only two. The two species look very much alike, but one is
more yellowish-green than gray-green.

What's In a Name?

Where did the name peyote come from? No one knows for sure.
Some people think it came from the Aztec word *pepeyoni* or
pepeyon, which means "to excite." Others think it came from
another Aztec word, *pi-youtli,* for a small plant with medicinal
powers. The most widely accepted explanation is that it comes
from the Nahuatl word *peyutl* or *peyotl,* which means silk cocoon
or caterpillar's cocoon. Native people might have used this word
to describe the silky spot of fuzz in the center of a peyote plant.
Over the years peyote has also been called by many colorful common names—cactus pudding, dumpling cactus, turnip cactus,
tuna de tierra (earth cactus), dry whiskey, and devil's root.

A peyote plant beginning to flower is shown here.

Where Does Peyote Grow?

You might think that such a rugged-looking plant could grow almost anywhere. You would be partly right. Peyote grows only in the Chihuahan Desert, but the tough little cactus is not too particular about exactly where in the desert it grows. It is often found under shrubs, such as mesquite or creosote bush, but it also does fine in the open, with no shade or protection. It can grow in mud flats that get flooded in the rainy season. It has even been found growing in cracks on steep limestone cliffs.

In the United States the more common species, Lophophora williamsii, is found only along the Río Grande in western Texas. On the Mexican side of the Río Grande, the plant's range extends several hundred miles. The less common species, Lophophora diffusa, is found only in one small patch of high-elevation desert in the Mexican state of Queretaro.

A peyote plant can take as long as five years to grow to the size of a dime. Those who use it for religious ceremonies generally make a pilgrimage—a sacred journey—to obtain it. The Huichol people of Mexico still make peyote-gathering pilgrimages similar to the ones their ancestors made. Once a year groups of men and women make the three-hundred-mile trip. They are led by a shaman, a traditional priest. He acts as a go-between, helping humans and spirits communicate with one another. The shaman, the Huichol believe, knows how to contact the god Tatewari. In Huichol legend, it was Tatewari who led the first peyote-gathering expedition to the place the Huichol call Wirikúta. During the trip each person takes on the identity of one of the Huichol gods, using that god's name instead of his or her own.

Peyote Pilgrimages

The peyote-gathering journey is no lighthearted vacation. Everyone who goes must follow strict rules. Before leaving on the trip they go through a ritual, confessing their sins and purifying themselves. As each person confesses, the shaman makes a knot in a string for each sin. Later, the string is burned. The Huichol believe that making the difficult pilgrimage helps them receive guidance from the gods and brings blessings to their lives— health, children, rain, protection from evil, even good relations with their neighbors.

The travelers carry sacred, hourglass-shaped gourds that they use in rituals during the journey. On their backs the travelers strap round baskets that they will fill with peyote when they reach Wirikúta. They take very little food. Some people fast for the whole trip. Others fast for most of each day, having just a little food and water in the evening. In the old days the Huichol made the whole journey on foot. Now, they rent large trucks, but they still get out and walk for certain parts of the trip.

The trip can be dangerous. People may become weak from going without food and water while traveling in the hot desert. They might encounter rattlesnakes and thieves. Sometimes their trucks break down on remote roads where it is hard to find help. The Huichol travelers stop at sacred places along the route, where they leave offerings, make confessions, and perform purification rituals. Relatives waiting at home go through similar ceremonies.

Finally the travelers reach the place where peyote grows. Before they can search for peyote, there are more rituals and ceremonies. The shaman tells traditional stories about peyote. He chants and prays for protection. The travelers, too, offer prayers.

They light candles and raise them toward the sun. Anyone who has never hunted peyote before is blindfolded. Then the shaman finds the first peyote plant. Remember that the Huichol believe that corn, deer, and peyote all are forms of the same thing. The shaman shoots the peyote cactus with an arrow, just as he would shoot a deer. The travelers offer gifts to the peyote and pray for their gifts to be accepted.

They gather the peyote. The travelers cut off the tops of peyote plants—the peyote buttons—and carefully load the buttons into baskets. They eat some peyote, but bring most of it home, dried and strung into garlands. They also eat peyote flowers, believing that helps them find more peyote.

If the peyote hunters find a clump of peyote with an unusual shape, they consider it a sign from the gods. To them, the special clumps look like snakes, bowls, baskets, or crosses. The most prized clump is one that looks like a deer. The peyote gatherers also pay special attention to color variations in the peyote plants, which they associate with sacred places.

On the first night of the peyote hunt, the travelers have an all-night ceremony. Each person eats peyote five times during the night, as the shaman and his assistants sing and tend a sacred fire. At dawn people paint designs on one another's faces with a yellow powder made from the root of a desert plant. At certain times during the pilgrimage, people exchange peyote that they have selected as carefully as you might choose a gift for a special friend. Sometimes they offer the peyote without saying anything, but sometimes they tell each other, "Chew it well, so that you will see your life."[5]

Before starting for home, the travelers have another ceremony. Arrows are placed on the ground, pointing north, south, east,

The Huichol people of Mexico make a long, difficult journey every year to a place called Wirikúta, to gather peyote.

and west. At midnight the travelers build a fire, and the shaman takes out some tobacco. Praying, he puts the tobacco near the fire, touches it with feathers, and then gives some to each traveler. The travelers put the tobacco in their sacred gourds.[6]

Back at home, the Huichol use some peyote in their own ceremonies. They sell some to the Cora and Tarahumara people, who also have peyote ceremonies, but do not go on pilgrimages.[7]

In the United States most Native Americans who use peyote live far from where it grows. In the past some made peyote-hunting pilgrimages. Like the Huichol, they had rules and rituals for peyote gathering. When they arrived at the place where peyote grew, they chose a leader, who directed their ceremonies. Usually they rolled and smoked tobacco cigarettes and prayed, asking the peyote to let them know where to find it. When they found the first plant, they prayed over it and placed their cigarette butts in a circle around it. Some believed that this plant then told them where to find more.

Various Native American groups have their own lore about how to find peyote plants. The Lipan Apache, for example, used to say:

> If you are having a hard time finding them, you do this: when you find just one by itself you eat it. When it takes effect, when you get a little dizzy, you will hear a noise like the wind from a certain direction. Go over there . . . from the place where the noise is coming, you will get many peyote plants.[8]

Licensed Peyote Dealers

Nowadays most Native Americans do not gather their own peyote. They can buy dried peyote buttons from a handful of people who are licensed to collect peyote and sell it to Native Americans. In 1996 there were nine licensed peyote dealers, called peyoteros, in the United States. All nine lived in western Texas, in and around the towns of Mirando City, Rio Grande City, and Oilton.[9]

In a *Los Angeles Times* article, reporter Louis Sahagun described a harvesting trip near Mirando City, Texas, with a peyotero named Salvador Johnson:

> *Against a backdrop of rolling desert spiked with thornbush and mesquite, Salvador Johnson used a shovel to scoop up a mind-bending cactus that pops out of the ground like biscuits in this part of West Texas. "Mira no más! [Look no further] Here's a whole family of them," Johnson said as he filled a bucket with cactus tops lopped off at ground level to protect their turnip-like root. "Save the root and . . . with a good rain, they'll be knockin' on the door to be harvested again."*[10]

A peyotero pays about four hundred fifty dollars for federal and state permits, which must be renewed every year. To get a permit, a person must have notarized letters of recommendation from local police, the federal Drug Enforcement Administration, and the Texas Department of Public Safety.

A permit is not all a peyotero needs. He or she also needs to be tough and a bit brave. Peyote grows on rocky hillsides in hot, dry country where rattlesnakes and stinging insects live. Peyoteros use sharp shovels or special tools to slice off the peyote buttons, leaving the roots. Then they take the peyote buttons home and spread them out to dry. Collecting peyote is not an easy job, and it does not bring in a lot of money—only about one hundred fifty dollars per one thousand buttons. Altogether, peyoteros sold 2,184,144 peyote buttons for $240,674 in 1995.[11] Still peyoteros like their work.

"It's a good job—it keeps you busy. For me, it's fun," says Isabel Lopez, who has been selling peyote for thirty years and even hands out business cards that read "Isabel M. Lopez, Peyote Dealer."[12]

Prices may go up in the future, as peyote becomes more scarce. Peyoteros have been harvesting peyote from the same places for years, and the demand for peyote is increasing. Most of the peyote grows on land owned by ranchers, and peyoteros must pay the landowners a fee to harvest the cactus. Some ranchers lease parts of their land to peyote pickers. But ranchers complain that peyoteros and their employees sometimes trespass on their land, looking for places to harvest more peyote without paying. Salvador Johnson, the peyotero who was featured in the *Los Angeles Times* article, once had his peyote dealer's permit suspended because one of his employees was caught trespassing.[13]

Because of the demand for peyote, some peyoteros have started picking more frequently. This means the plants do not have as much time to grow between harvests, so smaller and smaller peyote buttons are being harvested. Twenty-five years ago peyoteros picked only buttons that were more than two inches across. Now they pick one-inch buttons.

Farmers have started plowing some peyote fields to grow grass for cattle to eat. The plows they use rip the peyote plants

Licensed peyote dealer Isabel Lopez, shown here with harvested peyote buttons, says she enjoys her work.

out of the ground, roots and all. This practice is making peyote even more scarce.

The Drug Enforcement Administration worries that, as peyote becomes more scarce, Native Americans may start substituting the more dangerous drug phencyclidine (PCP) for peyote in their ceremonies. Native American Church leaders say this is not likely, but PCP is a very dangerous drug and this is a serious concern. "If you are truly members of the church, the peyote is the only one that you're supposed to use," explains Robert Billy Whitehorse, a leader in the Native American Church of Navajoland.[14]

The Native American Church would like to buy some of the peyote fields in Texas so members could harvest their own peyote. Another option would be to work out an agreement with the Mexican government that would let Native Americans harvest peyote in Mexico and bring it back across the border. Still it may take years to work out such an arrangement or to raise the money to buy land. For now church leaders are working with local landowners to make sure the peyote is protected and properly harvested.

Native Americans can buy peyote buttons through the mail, but some still prefer to travel to peyote country to buy their supplies directly from peyoteros. Every February about one thousand Native Americans, including officials of the Native American Church, come to Mirando City, Texas, to buy peyote and worship near the land where peyote grows.

When Native Americans visit peyoteros to buy peyote, they do not just pay for it and leave. Often they have a little ceremony, waving an eagle's feather over the peyote and smoking tobacco. Some peyoteros set up small shrines in their yards, where peyote buyers can pray. One former peyote dealer, an elderly woman named Amada Cardenas, has let peyote buyers camp and hold peyote ceremonies on her land for decades. Grateful for her hospitality, the Native Americans call her "Mom" or "Grandmother." Cardenas has even willed part of her land to the Native American Church, so the travelers will still have a place to stay and worship after she dies.[15]

In the past some buyers would visit the fields where the peyote had been harvested. There they would pray over the first peyote plant that was cut, then roll and smoke a tobacco cigarette to bless the plant. Since most peyote fields are on private property, however, it is becoming more difficult to visit them.

How Peyote is Used

Native Americans eat peyote buttons or make tea by boiling the cactus in water. The buttons can be eaten fresh or dried. Some people chew and swallow them right away. Others hold the buttons in their mouth for a long time, chewing them slowly. A typical dose is six to twelve buttons, but some people eat thirty or more. Peyote buttons have a very bitter taste—like a mixture of dirt and dried orange rinds. To make the peyote easier to eat, Native Americans sometimes grind the dried buttons into powder and eat it with a spoon. They can also mix the powder with a little water to make a paste, then form it into balls or pellets. Non-Native American users may take peyote in these forms, but they often try other methods to avoid getting sick. Some put fresh or dried peyote in a gelatine dessert and swallow spoonfuls whole.

Some peyote dealers set up small shrines in their yards where Native Americans can pray when they come to buy peyote.

Used in these ways, peyote does not need any special processing. But to extract the main active ingredient, mescaline, from peyote, several steps are necessary. "Underground chemists"—people who extract mescaline for illegal use—start by boiling fresh or dry peyote buttons. Then they go through a series of steps, adding different chemicals, such as lye, benzene, and sulfuric acid. Eventually needlelike white crystals settle out. The crystals are mescaline sulfate. The chemists dry the mescaline sulfate and purify it further.

In the 1960s, when many young people experimented with mind-altering drugs, Texas had trouble with unauthorized people raiding the peyote fields. Some of these people even set up crude outdoor labs to extract mescaline from peyote on the spot.

Mescaline also can be made from scratch in a laboratory. It was first done by Ernst Spath in 1919. Since then, other chemists have modified Spath's technique or come up with new ways of making synthetic mescaline. One researcher, Alexander Shulgin, has been making and experimenting with drugs similar to mescaline since the 1960s, when he was a chemist with the Dow Chemical Company. He invented a group of drugs called methoxyamphetamines, which are combinations of mescaline and amphetamines. The drug MDMA, sometimes called Ecstasy, is one example. Underground chemists have learned to make some of Shulgin's creations to sell illegally on the street.

A dose of 350 to 500 mg of mescaline—which can be taken as a powder, an aspirin-sized tablet, a capsule, or a liquid—produces effects that last five to twelve hours. In capsule form, mescaline sells for three to four dollars per capsule on the street.

To a chemist, mescaline is interesting because its structure is similar to that of norepinephrine, an important natural chemical found in the human body. Norepinephrine is a neurotransmitter—a chemical messenger that helps nerve impulses travel throughout the body. It plays an important role in the "fight or flight" response—the rapid heartbeat, increased blood pressure, dilated pupils, increased body temperature, and general excitement that automatically occur in stressful situations. Mescaline causes these same effects. The structure of mescaline is also similar to two other neurotransmitters, dopamine and serotonin.

Mescaline belongs to a group of chemical compounds called alkaloids. Alkaloids are found in certain plant families. Some are highly poisonous and some have medicinal uses. Many alkaloids have mind-altering effects. Cocaine, morphine, nicotine, and the poison strychnine all are alkaloids.

Fact and Fiction About Peyote

Some people believe that the white hairs in the center of a peyote button contain the poison strychnine, but that is a myth. The peyote cactus contains no strychnine.[16] Peyote does contain more than fifty different alkaloids, however. In 1888, German pharmacologist Louis Lewin extracted the first alkaloids from dried peyote samples.

A few years later, another German pharmacologist named Arthur Heffter got some fresh peyote from European cactus dealers and extracted four more peyote alkaloids. In those days researchers did not realize it might be dangerous to experiment on themselves with the drugs they were studying. Heffter tried each alkaloid on himself and discovered that only one of them made him have the kinds of hallucinations that peyote users had reported. He named that alkaloid mescaline. He used that name because people used to confuse peyote with mescal—an alcoholic beverage made from the century plant—and with mescal beans, the red seeds of a plant in the bean family.

The red mescal beans contain a chemical called cytisine. It causes nausea, convulsions, hallucinations and even death. Like peyote, mescal beans have been used by Native Americans and Mexicans for medicine and in ceremonies. The leaders of peyote ceremonies sometimes wear mescal bean necklaces.

Mescaline has also been found in at least four other kinds of cactus. Some other alkaloids found in peyote are found in other kinds of cactus, too. Still peyote contains more alkaloids than any other kind of cactus.

Other Kinds of Cactus

Next to peyote, the San Pedro cactus (Trichocereus pachanoi) is probably the best-known mescaline-containing cactus. It grows naturally in the Andes Mountains of South America, and people in Bolivia, Ecuador, and Peru grow it in gardens. Like peyote, San Pedro cactus has been used by Native Americans for a long time. Archeologists have found evidence that it was used more than three thousand years ago. Native tribes in some parts of South America still use San Pedro cactus in healing ceremonies. They slice it and boil it for hours to produce a drink called cimora. Folk healers called curanderos use cimora in rituals to find out what is making a person sick. Other people also use the drink to foretell the future.

Non-native users in other parts of the world use San Pedro cactus as a drug. They prepare it similarly, cutting it up and boiling it for many hours. Then they drink the thin, green liquid, which tastes something like liquid dish soap. If they can keep it down—and many people cannot—they have visions similar to the ones peyote produces.

Why do you suppose a plant would produce such potent, mind-altering chemicals? Do alkaloids somehow help the plant survive? Scientists have been looking for answers to these questions for a long time, and they have not agreed on answers. All alkaloids contain nitrogen. Maybe, scientists reason, alkaloids are a waste product—a plant's way of getting rid of excess nitrogen. But if that is true, why don't all plants contain alkaloids? Many alkaloids are poisonous, especially in large doses. Perhaps they protect the plant from being eaten by animals. But nature has a way of getting around such obstacles. Animals that eat the plants have evolved to be immune to the poisons.

For now, no one is sure why the hardy little peyote plant produces mescaline or other alkaloids. Scientists know much more, however, about how peyote and its ingredients affect the mind and body. In the next chapter, you will find out what they have learned.

Questions for Discussion

1. Do you agree or disagree that a peyote pilgrimage is a religious experience? Support your answer.

2. Do you think peyoteros should have legal authority to sell peyote? Why? Why not?

3. What are some possible explanations for why the peyote plant produces such a powerful, mind-altering chemical as mescaline?

3

Effects of Peyote

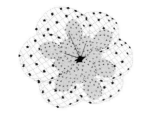

Devil's root or divine herb? People have used both names to describe peyote. How could one plant have a reputation for being both heavenly and horrible? Maybe it is because peyote's effects are hard to predict. Many things seem to influence how a peyote user will be affected—when and where the person takes peyote, the size of the dose, and what form the peyote is in are all factors. The user's personality, mood, past drug experience, and expectations of what is going to happen also seem to play a part. This is also described as the user's "set." Even in the same person, the effects can vary from one experience to the next. A person may have a good experience one time, but a terrifying bad trip the next. In fact, the experience can suddenly change from positive to negative during a single episode of use. There is no way to predict whether the effects will be good or bad, even in an experienced user.

Perhaps that helps explain why Native Americans and native Mexicans who use peyote in religious ceremonies consider it a route to God, while people who use it just to get high may have very unpleasant experiences. Although people's reactions to peyote vary, most users go through two stages after taking it.

Stage One

First comes a period of almost unbearable physical discomfort—nausea, vomiting, sweating, dizziness, headache. The user may feel too hot or too cold and may start to shake. Some have trouble breathing or feel like they are choking. Pains in the chest, neck, and stomach may be part of the reaction. Muscles may feel weak, and parts of the body may feel numb. Heart rate and blood pressure rise. With these uncomfortable physical sensations comes psychological discomfort—feelings of uneasiness, restlessness, depression, anxiety, and fear. Some users get so agitated that they become violent. These awful feelings start about an hour after taking peyote and last for three or four hours. Some people say it is like having a hangover *before* getting drunk.

Stage Two

In the second phase most of the discomfort eases, although some users still feel an odd mixture of depression and dreaminess. The body becomes uncoordinated and almost numb, yet the user may think he or she has unusual physical abilities. Sometimes there is a sensation of weightlessness or just the opposite—feeling very heavy. The pupils of the eyes open wide and hardly react to light. The most obvious effect, though, is that reality becomes blurred and distorted. The senses, especially sight and hearing, get scrambled. Not everyone has visions or hallucinations, but many users do. Usually the visions are not true hallucinations, but just distortions of reality. Researchers call these "pseudohallucinations," which means false hallucinations.

Ordinary objects start to look strange. Sometimes they seem to change shape, take on brilliant colors, or pulsate. Some users see complex geometric patterns, such as spider webs, tunnels, and spirals, but others see only simple shapes, colors, and flashes of light. Havelock Ellis, an English psychologist who wrote a detailed account of his mescaline experience in 1897, described "a vast field of golden jewels, studded with red and green stones, ever changing."[1] Shadows from the gaslight in his room seemed to be tinged with red, green, and violet.[2]

At first, users may see visions only when they close their eyes. As the experience progresses, some people see start to see more complicated, realistic visions—such as animals, people, and buildings—even with their eyes open. At first these are familiar scenes and faces, then they become unfamiliar.

Christopher Koenigsberg, who tried peyote several times as a young man in the mid-1970s, recalls that his hallucinations sometimes took the form of "little individual creatures, faces with personality and history and dignity behind them."[3]

Arthur Kleps, a psychologist, gave this description of a 1960 mescaline experience:

All night, I alternated between eyes open terror and eyes closed astonishment. With eyelids shut I saw a succession of elaborate scenes which lasted a few seconds each before being replaced by the next in line. Extra-terrestrial civilizations. Jungles. Organic computer interiors. Animated cartoons.

45

*Abstract light shows. Temples and palaces of a decidedly
pre-Colombian American type.*[4]

The kinds of visions a person sees and the way the person
interprets them depend on that person's background and culture.
An American college student might see visions that seem like
music videos, while a Huichol shaman might see deer, corn, candles, and Huichol gods.

Even within the same culture, family, group, or town, people
may have very different kinds of visions. The Huichol believe
that a person's visions depend on his or her spiritual awareness. A
shaman who has reached a high level of spirituality may see the
god Tatewari. People who are not as far along on their spiritual
paths will see only rattlesnakes, lizards, and mountain lions,
which they consider to be Tatewari's messengers.[5]

Some users have "auditory hallucinations"—they think they
hear sounds that are not really there. Even the boundaries
between the senses become blurred—a user may have the sensation of "hearing colors" or "seeing sounds." This blending of the
senses is called synesthesia.

Christopher Koenigsberg remembers feeling "lots of tingles
and chills, up and down the spine, even up and down the legs,
everywhere there were nerves . . . sometimes these blended with
and turned into hallucinations."[6] For the English psychologist
Havelock Ellis, smells blended with sights. He wrote that
". . . the air around me seemed flushed with vague perfumes, producing with the visions a delicious effect . . . ."[7]

It may sound like a pleasant experience, but it can actually be
quite confusing and upsetting. Although Koenigsberg saw pleas-
ing patterns of soft, pastel colors and felt "extremely wise and

Background and culture of the user influence the kinds of visions a person sees while under the influence of peyote. This yarn painting, by Huichol artist Cristobal Gonzalez, was influenced by peyote visions. It depicts symbols that are important in Huichol culture.

mature" at the beginning of his peyote trip, the experience soon turned into his first bad trip. As he tells it, "The tingles and chills turned into horrible scary flutters. Rugs and grass and dirt would erupt with all sorts of tiny little creatures."[8]

During this phase old memories may come flooding into the mind. They may be so vivid and realistic that they blend with whatever is really happening at that moment. This can lead the user to lose touch with the "here and now" and to lose the ability to tell the difference between what is real and what is not.

One of the most bizarre and disturbing effects is something called "depersonalization." The user starts to feel that his or her mind and body are not connected. It's almost like being two people at the same time. Here is how writer William Braden described it:

> I looked down at my tweed jacket and my green-and-white striped shirt, then farther down at my crossed legs. Black pants, black socks, black shoes. The only trouble was, the legs weren't mine. They looked alien and somehow sinister. I knew they were attached to my body, and I knew I could move them, but they weren't my legs. They weren't me. Or better yet, I wasn't them.[9]

Another user, a subject in an experiment conducted by two European researchers in the 1930s, had this unsettling experience:

> I drew my hand across my face and it felt as if the hand had no connection with me and did not belong to me. I looked at it as if it was not my own, then the feeling faded and not even by using my imagination could I recapture it.[10]

During this phase thoughts fly through the user's mind at a blinding pace. Instead of feeling fuzzy-headed, like someone who has had too much alcohol to drink, a peyote user has a feeling of keen awareness. But the rapid thoughts move too fast for the user to really stop and consider any of them. It is difficult to concentrate and easy to be distracted. Although the mind is full of thoughts, the user has trouble communicating them. Sometimes, this is because the user is too preoccupied with internal thoughts to even want to talk. It may also be because the user thinks he or she has already said something that he or she actually has only thought.

Withdrawing into himself or herself, the user even loses interest in getting up and moving around. Some people may simply feel lazy, but others say they feel temporarily paralyzed. The emotions, too, can seem frozen, leaving the user unable to feel happiness or sadness. Author R.C. Zaehner described the experience: "The inability to feel suddenly became alarming in the extreme. Had the drug merely paralyzed my emotions, I wondered, or had it perhaps destroyed them forever? Life without them would be unbearable."[11]

Instead of feeling numb, some users feel very emotional, swinging back and forth from giddiness to depression. These emotional extremes, coupled with the sense of mental sharpness, make some users believe they are having a meaningful, mystical experience. Even though reality is distorted, they may start to think that what they are experiencing is more "real" than reality. In this state of mind, users sometimes attach significance to things that really are meaningless. Or they start to believe things that later seem ridiculous—that they can communicate with animals, for example.

Ben Winton, an Arizona newspaper reporter who is one-quarter Yaqui Indian, once took peyote during a Native American Church ceremony and wrote about his experience. At the beginning of the meeting, people were singing in a language he did not recognize. Yet as the peyote took effect, Winton began to think he could understand the meaning of the songs. Soon, he recalled, "I felt I could sing in any language I wanted, and everyone there would understand."[12]

During a peyote experience, time and space seem to become distorted. Time seems to drag on or stand still. A minute can seem like a hundred years. People seem to be talking too slowly. There's a sort of Alice-in-Wonderland sensation, with things and people seeming too big one moment, and too small the next. Sometimes it is the user himself or herself who feels too big or too small. Psychiatrist and drug researcher Humphrey Osmond recalled that, "at one moment I would be a giant in a tiny cupboard, and the next, a dwarf in a huge hall."[13] Things that are standing still seem to be moving, and things that are moving seem to be standing still, or moving jerkily like actors in an old silent movie.

With so many odd and unfamiliar sensations, it is no wonder that some peyote and mescaline users get very upset. Panic, paranoia, and sheer terror are some of the feelings users have reported. In one study of thirty-four teenagers who said they had used mescaline (or something they thought was mescaline), fifteen said they had bad reactions, including panic, severe headaches, and terrifying hallucinations.

"No words can describe the appalling mental torment that continued for well over an hour," one mescaline user wrote. "There seemed no hope of being able to escape this torture—certainly for many hours, perhaps forever. Hell itself could hardly be more terrifying."[14]

When the British author Aldous Huxley took mescaline, he felt as if his whole personality was falling apart, and that made him panic.[15] Another user was terrified by his visions of "a wild black figure chopping off heads, because it was so funny to see them fall."[16] The awful visions are so frightening that some peyote users think they are about to die.

After seeing such visions and feeling the fear, panic, and suspicion peyote can create in their minds, some users say they understand what it must be like to be insane. In fact, peyote may produce reactions so similar to schizophrenia, researchers once thought that they could use peyote to help them understand the mental disorder. Both peyote and schizophrenia distort the senses, and can cause delusions, depersonalization, terror, and paranoia. When a person who actually has schizophrenia takes peyote or mescaline, the person's symptoms may become much worse. Instead of having pleasant feelings, the person becomes extremely anxious.

A person who starts to panic after taking peyote or mescaline should never be given sedatives, tranquilizers, or other drugs. A better idea is to help the person calm down and remember who and where he or she is. This is best done by someone who has experience working with drug users, such as a counselor at a drug crisis center. A user should never be left alone during a panic attack.

Native Americans and Mexicans who use peyote ceremonially can also have bad reactions. As far back as the seventeenth century, Spanish Jesuits reported that native people who used peyote saw "horrible visions."[17] This is similar to a "bad trip" after taking LSD. In the late 1800s, one person who studied the Huichol people reported that "in a few cases a man may consume so much that he is attacked with a fit of madness, rushing backward and forward, trying to kill people, and tearing his clothes to pieces."[18] A Winnebago man named Crashing Thunder described a peyote experience in which he thought he actually died and left his body. People who were with him during the experience were frightened, because they thought he had gone insane.[19]

Because of their beliefs and the setting in which they use the drug, Native Americans and native Mexicans usually interpret any negative reactions to peyote as part of the religious experience. If they get sick and throw up, they may see it as punishment for their sins. Many Huichol and Native American peyotists say that eating peyote is "tasting oneself." To a good, pure person, the peyote is not bitter, and it does not cause vomiting.[20] They also believe the bad reactions—and even the visions peyote produces—are signs that the body is being cleansed of impurities and evil spirits, which can cause illness.[21] To them, it is sort of like taking medicine that tastes so bad it makes you shudder. You hate it at the time, but you do it because you think it will help you get well. Some Native Americans also say the longer a person has used peyote for religious purposes, the less likely the person is to get sick.[22] They are developing a physical tolerance to it over time.

One study of peyote use by Navajo members of the Native American Church estimated that negative psychological reactions—bad trips—happened only about once in every seventy thousand times peyote was taken. This rate is much lower than what is usually found with other hallucinogenic drugs. The

In the controlled setting of a Native American peyote ceremony, bad trips are rare. But using peyote in other situations can be dangerous.

researcher who did the study believed the rate was lower among the Navajo because they use peyote only in the controlled setting of the peyote ceremony. Also the emotions that peyote releases are carefully channeled into positive directions during the Native American Church peyote ceremony. During the ceremony, things happen at specific times. That helps bring people back in touch with reality when their sense of time has been distorted. The roadman is trained to pay special attention to anyone who seems withdrawn or upset, and no one leaves until the effects of peyote have worn off.

How Does Peyote Work?

Just how do peyote and mescaline cause their strange effects? Peyote and mescaline are classified as psychedelic drugs, along with LSD and psilocybin, which comes from certain mushrooms. The term psychedelic was coined in the 1960s by the psychiatrist Humphrey Osmond. The word comes from the Greek word for "mind manifesting." It is used to describe drugs whose effects are mainly psychological, rather than physical— drugs that act on thought, perception, and mood. Such drugs are also called hallucinogens, which means hallucination-producing.

Scientists classify hallucinogens into different "families," based on the chemical structures of their active ingredients. Mescaline is in the phenylethylamine family. Other street drugs in the same family go by the names MDA, PMA, TMA, STP, Ibogaine, and MDMA. The chemical structures of phenylethylamines are similar to those of amphetamines.

Although mescaline is not in the same family as LSD and is much less potent than LSD, the two drugs produce almost identical effects. Since mescaline is less potent, it is usually taken in larger doses. A typical dose of mescaline is about one-third to one-half a gram, while a typical dose of LSD is only a few hundred thousandths of a gram. This may be why mescaline producers in the United States during the 1970s mixed mescaline and LSD. This mixture was commonly sold as "mesc" microdots. Something about the combination of alkaloids in peyote seems to produce stronger effects than when mescaline is taken alone.

Altering the Brain's Function

Some scientists think hallucinogens may alter pathways in the brain. That could explain why the senses seem to melt together, producing such bizarre effects as "seeing sounds" or "hearing colors." Yale University neuroscientist George Aghajanian has another possible explanation. He found that input from all the senses—sight, sound, smell, taste, and touch—makes neurons (nerve cells) fire faster in a part of the brain called the locus coeruleus. In experiments with animals, the neurons fired even faster when the animal had been given mescaline or another hallucinogenic drug. Since the locus coeruleus integrates messages from all the senses, it stands to reason that the increased activity could somehow scramble those messages.

Those fast-firing neurons in the locus coeruleus might also explain the sense of heightened awareness that peyote and mescaline users say they feel. The neuron activity may stimulate the release of the neurotransmitter norepinephrine throughout the brain. You may recall from Chapter 1 that norepinephrine plays a part in the "fight or flight" response, increasing alertness and preparing the body to respond to emergencies. This increased alertness might make users more aware of the "inner self" that they do not usually notice.

You may wonder how a drug that gets swallowed and travels through the digestive system could have any effect on the brain. Here is how it works. After a user swallows peyote or mescaline, the drug is gradually absorbed in the digestive tract. From there, it enters the bloodstream. The blood rapidly carries the drug throughout the body. To pass from the bloodstream into the brain, a drug must cross what is called the "blood-brain barrier." The blood-brain barrier is a sort of filter that allows certain substances to enter the brain, but keeps others out. It helps to protect the brain from toxic materials. It also helps to prevent abrupt changes in brain chemistry. Mescaline does not penetrate this barrier very well, but enough mescaline gets into the brain to produce its effects.

The effects of peyote or pure mescaline usually wear off after eight to twelve hours, as the drug is eliminated from the body. Users do not usually take mescaline or peyote for many days in a row. That is because they develop a tolerance for the drug after using it for a few days—no matter how much they take, they feel no effects. Only by staying off the drug for several days can the user feel the original effects again. A person who has developed a tolerance to mescaline also will not be able to feel the effects of certain other hallucinogenic drugs, such as LSD and psilocybin, until the tolerance wears off. This effect is called cross-tolerance.

Like other psychedelic drugs, peyote and mescaline do not produce psychological or physical dependence. Unlike heroin, nicotine, alcohol, and cocaine, peyote and mescaline do not cause users to crave these drugs or suffer withdrawal symptoms when they stop using them. Psychological dependence is the root of drug addiction. Peyote and mescaline are not addictive.

Can they cause other kinds of harm, however? What about birth defects, for example? In lab experiments, animals that are given mescaline regularly are more likely to have babies with birth defects. Still, scientists have not yet found evidence that the same thing happens in people. One cause of birth defects is chromosome damage. By looking for chromosome damage in people who use drugs, scientists can get an idea whether the drugs might cause birth defects. In one study researchers compared chromosome damage in two groups of native Mexicans. One group had used peyote for generations, while the other group had not used peyote. There were no differences in the rates of chromosome damage between the two groups. Another study found no evidence of chromosome damage in Huichol who had taken peyote up to thirty-five times a year.[23]

No deaths are known to have been caused directly by peyote or mescaline. But using these drugs can still be dangerous. Because they distort reality, peyote and mescaline might lead a user to do something risky that he or she would not ordinarily do. While peyote may be safe in the controlled setting of a Native American peyote ceremony, think what might happen if a user tried to drive, ride a motorcycle, or operate a boat while under the influence of a drug that alters the perception of time and space.

Mescaline was blamed for this tragic incident reported in a medical journal in 1985:

> *Three people were seen at the bottom of a steep hill near the*
> *ocean. One of the three (the victim) left the group and ran*

*up the hill at a steady pace despite the distance and the
steepness. Upon reaching the top, the runner did not pause,
but rather leaped out into midair as if to do a swan dive,
falling some 600 feet to his death.*[24]

An autopsy showed mescaline in the victim's system.

There is another cause for concern, says Dr. Richard
Schwartz, a Georgetown University professor and former medical director of a drug rehabilitation program. "The mescaline
user may commit suicide to escape from terrifying hallucinations
or from the mental depression and exhaustion that sometimes
follow the use of hallucinogenic drugs."[25] Even if the user does
not do anything this drastic, he or she may continue to feel upset
by the experience long after it is over.

One of the biggest dangers is that people who think they are
taking peyote or mescaline may actually be taking something
else. Peyote and mescaline are rare outside the southwestern
United States. But drug dealers sometimes sell pieces of dried
cactus sprayed with PCP, passing it off as peyote. Much of what
is sold as mescaline is actually LSD or PCP. PCP, also known as
angel dust, is a very dangerous drug that alters the ability to think
clearly and makes people act unpredictably—sometimes violently. A person can remain confused and disoriented for up to
two weeks after taking an overdose of PCP. In some people this
state of confusion is followed by a period of severe mental dis-
turbance that can last weeks or months. Unlike peyote and
mescaline, PCP causes psychological dependence, and it can
cause convulsions or coma. Several deaths have been blamed on
PCP. Some were overdoses, but others were murders or suicides
triggered by the drug's effects on behavior.

It is risky to drive, ride a motorcycle, or operate watercraft under the influence of a drug that alters one's sense of time and space.

With all the unpleasant and potentially dangerous effects, why would anyone choose to use peyote or mescaline? In the next chapter, you'll learn why members of the Native American Church feel peyote brings them closer to God. What about other users? Some are searching for meaning in their lives or trying to escape something unpleasant. In the process, however, they may become more withdrawn, increasing their isolation and pain. In the long run, doctors and drug counselors warn, trying to solve problems by altering one's state of mind only gets in the way of coming to terms with the real world.

Questions for Discussion

1. People have used terms such as "devil's root" and "divine herb" to describe peyote. Why do you think such opposing descriptions apply to the same plant?

2. Scientists have observed that different cultures have very different visions following peyote use. Explain some possible reasons for the variation in visions among cultures.

3. Because of their beliefs, Native Americans and Mexicans usually interpret any negative reactions to peyote as part of a religious experience. Do you agree or disagree with this interpretation? Why?

4

Peyote and the Native American Church

It was a special night for Rex Harvey. He had just finished military basic training in San Diego, and the young Navy seaman soon would be joining the crew of the supply ship USS *Juneau*. Before shipping out, he had come home to Arizona. No doubt he wanted to see his family and friends one more time. Perhaps he wanted one last taste of his favorite home-cooked meals. There was an even more important reason, however, for coming back to the foothills of the Chuska Mountains. Rex Harvey had come to ask for prayers and songs to guide him through the next four years—peyote prayers and songs.

As Navajo members of the Native American Church, Harvey and his family saw the peyote ceremony as an essential part of any major event in life. Believing that peyote is a gift from God, Native American Church members use it only in special prayer meetings that are held for specific purposes—to remember someone who has died; to mark a marriage or birth; to cure the sick; to give thanks for recovery from an illness; to celebrate Christmas, Thanksgiving, Easter, or the New Year; or to ask for help in a challenging or difficult situation. It is also used as a means to stop using other drugs, such as alcohol or heroin.

In an article in the *Arizona Republic*, reporter Jerry Kammer described the scene inside the tipi where Harvey's peyote meeting was held:

> *A fire before an earthen altar floods a [tipi] with golden light. Red embers ride a column of cedar smoke into the night's vast darkness. . . . Twenty-eight men and seven women sit cross-legged on the vermilion earth between the [tipi's] canvas arc and the long, slender crescent of the altar, which was sculpted that afternoon from the red earth. . . . A priest, more commonly known to Native American Church members as a "roadman," fans the cedar smoke toward the faithful with an eagle-feather wand. They reach out with both hands to receive the blessing, patting it into their heads and chests.*[1]

The Peyote Ceremony

Wearing a white shirt, jeans, and moccasins, Harvey sat in front of the altar. On top of the altar was a button of peyote. At the beginning of the meeting, everyone prayed as they smoked tobacco rolled in corn husks. Then the roadman's assistant gathered the cigarette butts and piled them at either end of the altar. Now it was time to pass the peyote.

A bowl of chopped peyote was passed clockwise around the circle. One by one, people took turns eating spoonfuls of the bitter cactus. Next came a gallon jug of peyote tea. As someone beat a drum, the roadman shook a rattle with one hand. In his other hand was a feathered prayer stick. He began to sing songs with themes of strength, guidance, and protection. Then the drum, rattle, and prayer stick were passed around the circle, and each person took a turn singing. About once an hour the peyote was passed around again, and advice was offered to Harvey.

Twelve hours after the prayer meeting began, the sun peeked over the Chuska Mountains, and the meeting drew to a close. Harvey slipped away to a nearby relative's house, changed into his Navy uniform, and came back. The roadman gave him a special blessing, gathering smoke around him with the prayer fan. Harvey's mother brought in a bucket of water. The roadman blew an eagle-bone whistle four times, turning to face north, south, east, and west. He dipped his prayer wand into the bucket, and flicked water around the tipi and onto the fire. Then he handed the bucket to Harvey, who took a drink and passed the bucket around the circle. Finally Harvey's mother brought in bowls filled with chopped beef, corn, and fruit salad—the traditional meal served at the close of a peyote prayer service. Rex Harvey had been properly blessed. Now he was ready to serve his country.[2]

Rex Harvey's prayer meeting was held in 1993, but it was very much like the peyote ceremonies Native Americans have been holding since the late 1800s. As you read in Chapter 1, Native Americans learned about peyote from native Mexicans,

These prayer fans, made by roadman Anthony Davis/White Thunder, are used in Native American Church peyote ceremonies.

and the peyote ceremony quickly spread from tribe to tribe. Although early peyote ceremonies borrowed some Christian traditions, no one saw a need for a single, organized "peyote church" until 1918.

Native Americans had always had to defend their peyote use against people who thought it was evil, immoral, or unhealthy, but they were facing even greater opposition around 1918. White teachers, missionaries, Bureau of Indian Affairs officials, and even some Native Americans had been pressing to have peyote outlawed. In hearings before the United States House of Representatives, the peyotists had won the right to keep using peyote in their religious ceremonies. Yet they knew the fight was not over.

In the hearings, the peyotists had argued that their church was just like any other church—Baptist, Presbyterian, or Catholic. There were some big differences, however. The "peyote church" had no conventional name, officers, rules, or goals. While those things might not matter to the peyotists, they did matter to others. To be taken as seriously as other organized religions, the peyote church had to become an organized religion.

In August 1918, peyotists from several tribes met at El Reno, Oklahoma, to establish the Native American Church. The purpose, as stated in the church's official documents, was to:

> . . . *foster and promote the religious belief of the several tribes of Indians in the State of Oklahoma, in the Christian religion with the practice of the Peyote Sacrament . . . .*
> . . . *to teach the Christian religion with morality, sobriety, industry, kindly charity and right living, and to cultivate a*

spirit of self-respect and brotherly union among the members of the Native Race of Indians.[3]

As the peyotists had suspected, their struggle to defend ceremonial use of peyote still was not over. The Bureau of Indian Affairs sent questionnaires to reservations, schools, and hospitals, asking for evidence of the negative effects of peyote. The bureau published and distributed the results in an antipeyote pamphlet called simply *Peyote.* Although several attempts to pass a federal law against peyote failed, the legislatures of fourteen states outlawed peyote between 1899 and 1937.[4] Over the years the Native American Church became a strong force against those who opposed peyote use.

In the early days the Native American Church focused on attracting members from Oklahoma tribes. Eventually new churches were chartered in Nebraska, South Dakota, North Dakota, Montana, Idaho, Wisconsin, and Iowa. Finally in 1944 the name was changed to the Native American Church of the United States.

Today the church has many branches, such as the Native American Church of Navajoland, the Native American Church of Oklahoma, and the Native American Church of North America. More than two hundred fifty thousand Native Americans consider themselves members of the church, although not all of them are officially registered. Certain branches require registered members to be at least 25 percent Native American and to be known within their communities as upstanding citizens.[5] Other branches allow non-Native Americans to join.

Most Native American tribes have some people who support the peyote religion and others who do not. Although the

Native American Church is only one of many churches on most reservations, it is particularly popular among certain tribes, such as the Navajo. By the early 1980s about half of all Navajo were Native American Church peyotists.[6]

Peyote's Place in Native American Culture

To Native American Church members, peyote is not perceived as a drug. They believe that using peyote in religious ceremonies is something like drinking wine during the Christian ritual of communion. Both wine and peyote are drugs, however. While communion wine is a symbol of Christ's blood, peyote is more than a symbol to Native American Church members. It is not just a sign of the divine, peyote itself is divine, church members believe.[7] Peyote, they say, is a "comfort, healer, and guide" to the spiritual life—a direct link to God. Some call it "medicine," because they believe it can cure illness, purify the mind, nourish the soul, and help people know the difference between right and wrong. To Native Americans, "medicine" does not treat just the body. Because they believe that the body, mind, and spirit all are connected, their medicines work on all three at the same time. Some Native Americans also call peyote the "holy sacrament." Using peyote outside a religious ceremony is sacrilegious, many feel.[8]

"To us, peyote is the heart of God or the flesh of God," peyote roadman Reuben Snake once said. "Some churches can't practice their religion without bread and wine. We can't practice ours without peyote."[9]

Every peyote meeting has a specific purpose, and peyote is never taken just "to see what happens."[10] Ceremonies may vary slightly in different Native American communities, but the basics of the meeting are similar. Some are held in tipis; others, in traditional round, wooden chapels. A typical meeting begins on Saturday night and goes on all night long. People sit in a circle around a crescent-shaped altar, which curves around an open fire. For hours and hours they sit with their backs straight and their feet tucked underneath them. Sitting this way is a sign of respect and reverence. Sometimes a crucifix is placed on the altar, on top of a large, dried peyote button, called the "chief," the "father peyote," or the "grandfather peyote,"[11] A Bible is sometimes placed nearby.

A "grandfather peyote" button is considered a treasure and kept in a decorated box when it is not being used. Some are even collector's items. One prominent Kiowa peyote leader kept a peyote button that had belonged to the Comanche leader Quanah Parker. He would pass it around the circle at the end of peyote meetings, and everyone would handle it reverently.

The peyote ceremony is led by a roadman. The name roadman comes from the term "peyote road" —the path of righteous living that a peyotist tries to follow from birth until death. In the peyote ceremony a straight line running across the crescent-shaped altar symbolizes the peyote road.

In some ceremonies other officials help the roadman. The cedar man sprinkles ground cedar incense on the fire, the fire man tends the fire all night, and the drummer plays the ceremonial drum. Tobacco plays an important part in the ceremony. People smoke it or rub it on their bodies as they offer prayers. After these smoking rituals, the roadman takes a sprig of sagebrush,

"Peyote chiefs" or "grandfather peyote" buttons are treasured by Native American Church members.

waves it in the cedar smoke to bless it, and pats it on his forehead, chest, shoulders, thighs, and arms. Then he passes the sagebrush around the circle, and everyone does the same thing.

Peyote is passed around at certain times during the ceremony. It may be in the form of chopped or sliced fresh peyote; peyote tea; spoonfuls of dried, ground peyote; or little pellets or balls made from ground peyote. Some people have trouble swallowing peyote because it is so bitter. The muddy-tasting tea helps wash down the other forms of peyote.

After the first time peyote is passed around, the singing begins. The roadman starts the singing with a song that says, "May the gods bless me, help me, and give me power and understanding."[12] He repeats the song four times. As the roadman sings, the drummer beats a drum made from an iron or brass kettle with buckskin stretched over the top. The drum has water inside, and once in awhile, the drummer shakes the drum to moisten the buckskin. After the roadman has sung his opening songs, the drummer sings a group of four songs, as the roadman beats the drum. Next, the cedar man sings four peyote songs. Everyone else sits quietly, staring at the fire or the altar or praying softly. Instead of thinking about themselves, they are supposed to think about the purpose of the meeting and to ask God to hear their prayers. When all the officials have sung their songs, they pass the drum, rattle, and prayer stick around the circle, giving everyone a chance to sing their own sets of four peyote songs. Some peyote songs are stories in musical form; others are about nature or about peyote itself. There are songs about Jesus, songs of repentance, and songs of prayer. During the singing some people also shake rattles shaped like peyote buttons or play whistles shaped like birds.

At midnight there is a special ceremony with more songs and rituals. More cedar is sprinkled on the fire and the fire man goes outside to get a bucket of water. After the roadman blesses the water by blowing the eagle bone whistle and drawing it through the water, the bucket and cup are passed around the circle, and everyone can have a drink. After the midnight ceremony anyone who wants to can go outside to stretch. Then the ceremony continues until the first light of dawn. At dawn the roadman blows the eagle whistle four times, and a woman brings in another bucket of water. The roadman sings four morning songs, and the woman makes a cigarette, smokes it, prays, and passes it to the officials. They also smoke and pray.

If the purpose of the ceremony is to treat someone who is sick, the roadman performs a curing ritual. Then the water is passed around for everyone to drink. Finally the traditional breakfast of meat, fruit, and corn is passed around, and each person takes a handful. In some ceremonies there is a time after all the rituals when anyone who wants to speak can do so. People express gratitude for the meeting and promise to try to live better lives. Elders give advice about life to younger people. Then the roadman or fire man leads everyone out of the tipi. Around lunchtime there is usually a big feast for the participants and their families. People relax and socialize until time to go home.[13]

Using peyote in these all-night prayer meetings "gives you a good blessing for everyday life," says Robert Billy Whitehorse, a leader in the Native American Church of Navajoland. He says peyote broadens his thinking, helps him make wiser decisions, and makes him feel better about himself.

"It gives me a pride and an image of myself that I'm not going to sit there and wait for a handout," Whitehorse explains.

"I am going to go out and do. If somebody else can do, I can do it too. It gives that kind of thought and feeling that give me the courage to go. That all comes with the blessing."[14]

Scholars who have studied Native American peyotism generally agree that it is a serious, meaningful religion, not an excuse to get high. Edward Anderson, a botanist who studied peyote for many years, was impressed with the reverence of a Navajo peyote ceremony he attended in 1971. He wrote:

> *The seriousness of the Indians who participated was very impressive and obviously it was a meaningful and valid religious experience to them. It was not a dangerous orgy in which there was intoxication, sexual license, and other immoral activities. Peyotism demands much of its followers: physical endurance, patience, confession, and repentance.[15]*

In fact, Native American Church members claim that using peyote keeps them from doing things that are unwholesome, immoral, or illegal. Since the early days of the Native American peyote religion, there has been an emphasis on clean living and good behavior. Drinking alcohol, in particular, has been discouraged. Some Native Americans say peyote cures alcoholism. This may seem like substituting one drug for another. Native American peyotists, however, do not see it this way, because they do not perceive peyote as a drug.

In a letter he wrote to the Bureau of Indian Affairs in 1908, Winnebago peyotist and community leader Albert Hensley claimed that peyote "takes away the desire for strong drink . . . Hundreds of confirmed drunkards have been dragged from their downward way."[16]

After interviewing several Kaw (also called Kansa) peyotists in Kansas in 1914, one researcher reported, "The effect of peyote-eating on the Kansa has been to abolish drunkenness among its followers."[17] In response to a questionnaire sent out by the Bureau of Indian Affairs in 1909, several Indian agency superintendents made similar comments. In a 1919 report on Shoshone peyotists, another superintendent noted that "the members of the peyote lodge refuse to use whiskey, refuse to gamble, and altogether are among the better members of the tribe."[18]

More recently Dr. Robert L. Bergman, a public health physician who studied peyote use among the Navajo in the late 1960s and early 1970s, reported almost no negative effects. On the contrary, he found that religious use of peyote seemed to make people feel better about themselves and strengthen their bonds with other people. Commenting on the benefits he had observed, he wrote:

> We have seen many patients come through difficult crises with the help of this religion . . . It provides real help in seeing themselves not as people whose place and way in the world is gone, but as people whose way can be strong enough to change and meet new challenges.[19]

Speaking at a 1990 gathering of Native American leaders in Washington, D.C., Reuben Snake stressed that peyote, as used by the Native American Church, does not pose the kind of threat other drugs do.

> For the last twenty years, the American people have been suffering an epidemic of abuse of refined chemical drugs like cocaine, heroin, amphetamines, PCP, and so forth. American cities are crawling with violence and crime. This

is a terrible tragedy, and this kind of drug abuse is also a problem for some Indian youth.

But there is no peyote drug abuse problem. I defy the Justices of the Supreme Court to find newspaper reports of drive-by shootings in connection with the Holy Medicine. I challenge anyone concerned about the problem of drug abuse to find examples of dope peddlers selling the Holy Medicine in America's school yards and play grounds. The idea is preposterous. We don't have a peyote abuse problem in this nation.[20]

Native American Peyote Use is Not Recreational

Native American Church peyotists strongly oppose recreational drug use, and they do not approve of non-Native Americans using peyote to get high.

"It should be used only in a bona fide ceremony," says Robert Billy Whitehorse of the Native American Church of Navajoland. "We want to keep it like that, because if we don't, some people use it outside the church service and they just do whatever they want to do—they might be mixing it up with other drugs." During the annual peyote pilgrimage to Texas, Whitehorse has been upset to see non-Native Americans try to sneak in and steal peyote.

"They come to Texas and think they can get away with using the peyote as a drug," Whitehorse says. "They crawl over the fences or tear down the fences and uproot the whole thing and run off with it." He and the leaders of the other two main branches of the church are working with local ranchers to prevent such behavior.[21]

Legal Challenges to Peyote Use By Native Americans

In spite of the long history of ceremonial peyote use and the claims of its benefits, Native American peyotists have faced many legal challenges. In 1960, for example, a Navajo woman named Mary Attakai was arrested in Arizona for illegal possession of peyote. Her attorneys argued that her constitutional right to religious freedom had been violated. The judge agreed. In another case in California in 1962, police raided a peyote ceremony and arrested three Navajos. Again attorneys argued that the state law prohibiting peyote use interfered with religious freedom. This time the judge disagreed and found the three Navajos guilty. The three peyotists appealed the decision and lost again in appeals court.

Then the case went to the California Supreme Court, where the two earlier verdicts were overturned. The Supreme Court Justices decided that peyote use in "honest religious rites" was protected by the United States Constitution.[22] They also pointed out that law officers and courts "should have no trouble distinguishing between church members who use peyote in good faith and those who take it just for the sensations it produces."[23] The Court would probably make a similar decision today. Laws have since been passed that allow Native Americans to legally use peyote in religious ceremonies.

In 1978 Congress passed the American Indian Religious Freedom Act, a law intended to protect Native Americans' rights to own and use sacred objects and to worship through traditional ceremonies. That still was not the end of the battle, however. The act had no provisions for enforcement, and peyote possession continued to be against the law in many states.

A 1990 case in Oregon focused attention on the issue. Six years earlier Alfred L. Smith and Galen W. Black had been fired from their jobs as drug rehabilitation counselors for using peyote in Native American Church ceremonies. Both men were members of the church. Smith was a member of the Klamath tribe; Black was not a Native American. Officials of the drug abuse program where they worked said they violated the rule that employees must be drug-free. Although the men had been warned they would be fired if they used peyote at church, they felt it was a necessary part of their religion. "It doctors me in a good way," Smith said in a 1989 newspaper interview. "I sing. Sometimes I cry. It just touches an inner spirit and awareness."[24]

Black and Smith filed for unemployment benefits, but they were turned down because they had been fired for breaking the law. The two men claimed that the law did not apply to them because they were simply exercising their right to religious freedom. For the next six years the case bounced from one court to another. At one point the Oregon Supreme Court ruled that ceremonial use of peyote in the Native American Church was permissible under state law. To prohibit it would violate the rights of religious freedom guaranteed by the First Amendment to the Constitution, the Justices said.[25] Yet when the case finally went to the United States Supreme Court, which had the final say in 1989, that Court disagreed. Since the Oregon law was not passed specifically to prevent Native American Church members from using peyote, it did not violate their rights, even though it made their religious practices illegal, the Justices reasoned.[26]

The Supreme Court decision concerned leaders of many religious groups, both Christian and Jewish. They worried that their own religious freedom might be threatened. Along with the Native American Church, a group of about fifty religious and civil liberties organizations began pushing for a law that would guarantee everyone the right to practice their religion. Finally on October 6, 1994, President Bill Clinton signed the American Indian Religious Freedom Act Amendments of 1994, making it legal for Native Americans to possess, use, or transport peyote for ceremonial purposes. The law also protects Native Americans from being penalized or discriminated against because they use peyote.

In the United States today, only Native Americans from federally recognized tribes can legally use peyote. They can use it only in traditional Native American religious practices. In Canada the rights of native people to use peyote have not been established.

Questions for Discussion

1. Do you think it is appropriate for military personnel to participate in peyote ceremonies? Why? Why not?

2. Do you think it is fair that Native Americans have always had to defend their right to use peyote as part of their religion? Why? Why not?

3. Some Native Americans believe that peyote takes away one's desire to drink. Do you agree or disagree with this idea? Why? Why not?

5

Peyote and Society

With its long and complex history, peyote has affected individuals and groups of people in many different ways—some good, some bad. You have already read about the ways Native Americans have used peyote and how it has affected their culture. Now we will look at ways that other people have used peyote and mescaline and how these uses affect society.

For a long time non-Native Americans had little interest in using peyote. Occasionally a curious anthropologist or Bureau of Indian Affairs superintendent would try it, just to try to understand why it was so important to the Native Americans with whom they worked. During the Civil War imprisoned Texas Rangers resorted to using peyote because they had no alcohol to drink. They soaked the peyote, which they called "white mule," in water and got drunk on the liquid.[1]

Medical Benefits of Peyote

As Native American peyote use spread, physicians started hearing claims of the drug's medicinal properties. Native American users claimed peyote could cure everything from toothaches to tuberculosis. In the late 1800s doctors started trying peyote on themselves and their patients. Writing in the New York Medical Journal, one doctor reported that peyote had relieved a patient's headaches and neuralgia (nerve pain). He thought peyote might make a good substitute for morphine, a powerful, but addictive, painkiller.[2] We now know that it is not wise to substitute one dangerous drug for another.

Other doctors reported using peyote to treat abdominal pain, throat tickles, headaches, irritability, "general nervousness," and even color blindness. However, these early reports were not based on careful scientific studies. The small doses of peyote the doctors gave their patients probably were not even enough to cause any effects. Although a few doctors were enthusiastic about what they thought peyote could do, many others were skeptical, and peyote use never caught on in mainstream medicine.

Peyote Research Popular

In the 1950s and 1960s there was another surge of interest in peyote, and some researchers tried again to find scientific proof of its supposed medical benefits. Experiments at California State University, Fullerton, showed that peyote acted like an antibiotic. In a lab dish an extract of peyote inhibited the growth of eighteen penicillin-resistant strains of the bacterium Staphylococcus aureus. The extract had the same effect in mice infected with Staphylococcus aureus. Yet many plants contain compounds that kill or inhibit bacteria. Usually it is not worth developing them as medicines, because they do not work as well as antibiotics that are already on the market. Interest in peyote as an antibiotic died out, perhaps because other researchers were not able to get the same results that the California researchers did. Today there are no accepted uses for peyote or mescaline in mainstream medicine.

Since peyote affects the mind, some researchers have thought it might help them treat—or at least better understand—mental disorders. But the results of experiments have been contradictory, and scientists have developed other drugs that they believe work better. Some therapists have given mescaline to patients during psychotherapy sessions. They say the drug breaks down psychological barriers and makes the patient more open and spontaneous. It can even change a patient's outlook on life, some therapists have claimed. Other psychiatrists and psychologists say those claims are exaggerated. Any positive effects last only a short time and may not be due to the mescaline at all, they argue.

Research Ends

Today most research into using mescaline and other hallucinogens in psychotherapy has been phased out. In some cases the research ended because of negative public opinions toward hallucinogens. People associated those drugs with hippies, and thought it was not appropriate for respectable scientists to study them.

"There seemed to be an increasing hysteria about hallucinogenic drugs in the 1960s that essentially shut down the research," said Frank Vocci of the National Institute on Drug Abuse. "It became socially unacceptable to do this kind of work."[3]

In other cases the results just were not good enough to justify using drugs with such powerful psychological effects. Still some researchers feel that the possible benefits of hallucinogens have not been explored thoroughly enough.

In the early 1990s the Drug Enforcement Administration and the Food and Drug Administration granted permission for a few new studies on the effects of hallucinogens. Yet as of 1996 none of the studies involved peyote or mescaline. Some peyote and mescaline studies eventually may be done through a new research organization called the Heffter Research Institute. The institute is named for the German scientist who discovered in 1897 that mescaline was the active ingredient in peyote. The Heffter Research Institute's goal is to use strict scientific methods to study the effects and possible medical uses of hallucinogens.

One question that scientists at the Heffter Institute might try to answer is: "Do drugs like mescaline expand the mind or simply trick it?" When a person uses mescaline or peyote and has a feeling of being in touch with God and the universe, has something meaningful really happened? Or has the drug, through its action on the brain's chemistry and activity, just created the sense that something meaningful has happened? If these religious feelings come from chemical changes in the brain, are all religious feelings based on brain chemistry? These are tricky questions to try to answer.

Another tricky question relates to the influence of the Native American Church on alcoholism and good conduct. Peyote-using members of the church say peyote ceremonies help them stay sober and live wholesome, moral lives. Yet is their good behavior due to the church's influence, the peyote's influence, or a combination of the two? New York social psychologist Neal Goldsmith hopes to do a study that will shed light on the question.

Researchers and Native Americans also want to find out more about the safety of peyote use. How long after a peyote meeting should someone wait before driving? Is it safe for Native American Church members to use peyote while serving in the military? These questions all need to be answered.

Scientists and physicians are not the only people who have experimented with peyote and mescaline. In the 1960s and 1970s young people experimented widely with all sorts of illegal drugs. "Mind-expanding" hallucinogenic drugs, such as LSD, peyote, and mescaline, were especially popular. Some young people who became interested in these drugs had been volunteer subjects in university research on hallucinogens. In that controlled setting, some had pleasant experiences they wanted to repeat outside the lab, with friends. Users believed these drugs enhanced their appreciation of art and music, helped them explore their feelings, showed them solutions to problems, and led them to spiritual insights. At one point in the 1970s, 25 percent of young people in the eighteen-to twenty-five-year-old range said they used mescaline.[4]

A whole subculture grew out of this drug use, with its own codes of conduct, music, and vivid, "psychedelic" clothing styles. There were also colorful names for drugs—peyote was sometimes called "moon" or "the bad seed."[5] It was a time of great social change—and not just because of the drug craze. The civil rights movement, the Vietnam War, and other social issues stirred the passions of young people and created conflict between generations. Young people's open use of illegal drugs added to the conflict.

Laws Against Peyote Use

Until the 1960s there were no federal laws against peyote use. Then in 1965 Congress passed the Drug Abuse Control Amendments Act, making it illegal for anyone to possess, sell, or use peyote. However, the law made exceptions for religious use. In 1970 peyote and several other psychedelic drugs were placed under the United States Controlled Substances Act, which also allowed for Native American peyote use. Peyote and mescaline were classified as a Schedule I controlled substances, in the same category with LSD and marijuana. Schedule I drugs are considered to have a high potential for abuse, present an unacceptable safety risk, and have no acceptable medical use.

By the late 1970s illegal drug use began to drop. It was partly because the government had started a campaign against drugs, backed with extra money for law enforcement and drug treatment. Drug arrests increased from less than thirty thousand in 1963 to 233,000 in 1969.[6] The percentage of teenagers arrested for drug use jumped dramatically during the same time. In 1963 only 6 percent of all drug arrests involved teenagers under eighteen. By 1969 the figure was 25 percent. The stress of being arrested—or being afraid of being arrested—did not fit well with young people's ideals of peace and love. On top of that, many had negative experiences with drugs—from bad trips to money lost through bad drug deals. Whether disillusioned with drugs or simply ready to move on to another stage of life, many young people who used hallucinogens in the 1960s and 1970s eventually gave them up.

From its peak in 1969 total illegal drug use in the United States dropped steadily until 1992. Since 1992 the percentage of Americans using illegal drugs has remained fairly level—around

Hallucinogenic drug experiences influenced the brightly colored "psychedelic" clothing of the 1960s and 1970s.

5.5 percent to 6 percent.[7] How many of those people use peyote and mescaline illegally? It is hard to say. Most statistics on drug use look at all hallucinogens together. As of 1994 more than eighteen million Americans (8.7 percent of the population) had used hallucinogens in their lifetime. Among twelve- to seventeen-year-olds, 4 percent had tried hallucinogens at least once, and just over 1 percent were currently using hallucinogenic drugs. Among eighteen-to twenty-five year olds, 1.8 percent were currently using hallucinogens. However, LSD—not mescaline or peyote—is the most commonly used hallucinogen. Because mescaline and peyote are expensive and hard to find, they are seldom used by non-Native Americans. Peyote's unpleasant effects—nausea, vomiting, sweating, and panic attacks—also make it unpopular. Even in Texas, where peyote grows wild, it seldom figures in major illegal drug deals.

Is it Really Peyote?

When young people try peyote or mescaline, it is usually as an experiment, not as a habit. Often young people who think they are using mescaline or peyote are being fooled. In a survey of 174 teenagers in a drug treatment program, 18 percent had taken a drug they thought was mescaline. Yet from the way they described the drug and its effects, it was clear they had taken something else—probably LSD. Other research suggests that only 17 percent of pills and capsules sold on the street as mescaline actually contain that drug.[8] Most contain LSD, PCP, or a combination of the two. Taking a drug without knowing what it is increases the risk of having problems. In addition, most drugs in the LSD and mescaline family are made only in illegal labs for illegal use. The manufacturers do not guarantee their quality or purity, and often the drugs are mixed with other harmful substances. Drug experts warn that using drugs of this type is especially risky.

There are also legal risks. Except for Native American Church members and peyote dealers, anyone caught with peyote or mescaline is charged with illegal drug possession. The penalties are up to fifteen years in prison, a fine of up to $25,000, or both.[9]

What makes a person decide to try a hallucinogenic drug? There are many reasons. Some people see it as an adventure; some do it to be accepted by other users or because it makes them feel grown up. Just like any drug use, hallucinogen use can be seen as an escape from a difficult situation at home or school, as a way to rebel, or as a way to cope with unhappiness, depression, or boredom. Whatever the reason for starting, drugs are never the solution to anyone's problems.

People are more likely to try drugs if they believe they are not harmful, and many people believe hallucinogenic drugs, such as peyote and mescaline, are not dangerous.[10] Are they?

They can cause impaired judgment, which could lead to accidents or unwise decisions. They can also cause anxiety and depression. While these effects are only temporary, the user may not realize that. Studies have shown that lonely teenagers who use drugs are more likely than others to feel hopeless. Hopelessness can lead to suicide attempts.

Drug experts also worry about the effects of mescaline, peyote, and other drugs, when combined with alcohol. In the past drug users tended to specialize—they were heroin users or opium users, for example. Today it is more common to use many kinds of drugs at once, often combined with alcohol. This is known as polydrug use. In one study of teenage drug users, those who had used mescaline almost always used it along with other drugs, such as marijuana or alcohol.

Hallucinogenic drugs can also interact with prescription drugs in harmful and sometimes unpredictable ways. Mescaline, for example, is especially dangerous for diabetics who take insulin. A diabetic person who takes too much insulin may have a bad reaction, becoming nauseated, weak, nervous, shaky, confused, and sweaty. If the reaction is not treated quickly enough, the symptoms become worse and the person may have convulsions and collapse. Studies of rats show that mescaline increases the harmful effects of an insulin overdose.

Another concern is that making it legal for Native Americans to use peyote in religious ceremonies has opened the door for other people to claim they should have the right to use peyote or other hallucinogenic drugs in their own religions. Since the law allows peyote use only by enrolled members of federally recognized Native American tribes, some people feel the law is discriminatory. If peyote is safe and helpful to Native Americans, they argue, why should other people be denied its benefits?

The Peyote Way Church of God, which split off from the Native American Church in 1966 and allows members of all races, also uses peyote in its ceremonies, but without legal permission. The church tried for many years to get permission. Finally the Supreme Court ruled against the church. Other groups, such as the Church of the Tree of Life and the Church of the Awakening, also have been denied legal permission to use peyote.

Legal or not, people have always found ways to use peyote, mescaline, and other mind-altering drugs. Whether searching for God or simply seeking thrills, there have been drug users and abusers in almost every culture, throughout history. Does that mean that using drugs to alter one's consciousness is almost a basic human drive, like hunger or thirst? A few scientists have suggested that. However, drugs are not a necessary part of life. There are many other, legal ways of feeling good.

Drugs may provide a quick, temporary sense of well-being, but there are many other routes to feeling happy and even "high." As Dr. Andrew Weil and co-author Winifred Rosen point out in their book *From Chocolate to Morphine,* drugs do not contain highs. "Highs exist within the human nervous system; all drugs do is trigger highs or provide an excuse to notice them."[11] That means that non-drug methods of feeling good can be just as effective as drugs. Unlike drugs, these other methods usually produce longer-lasting effects.

Music, meditation, art, dance, sports, writing, outdoor activity—almost anything a person can get absorbed in—can bring on all sorts of good feelings that rival the highs of drugs. People accustomed to using drugs may have to work harder to feel good through other methods, but once they do, they may prefer natural highs.

In the 1960s Dr. Herbert Benson was studying the effects of meditation on blood pressure. He was not trying to show that meditation could substitute for drug use, but he made an accidental discovery. For his study he had recruited twenty young men who all practiced meditation for fifteen to twenty minutes a day. In asking the volunteers background questions, Benson discovered that nineteen of the twenty had used drugs before

Former drug users have found even better highs through meditation, outdoor activity, and other enjoyable pastimes.

taking up meditation. All nineteen said they had quit using drugs because drug experiences just could not compare to the good feelings they got from meditation.

Meditation may not be for everyone, but everyone can find something besides drugs that makes them feel good. Young people, in particular, need to think carefully about the ways they make themselves feel better. The teen years can be tough—no one denies that. Everything seems to be changing at once— your body, your self-image, your expectations of yourself, and the expectations others place on you. It is natural to want to escape the pressures sometimes.

Psychologists warn that using drugs during the teen years—whether peyote, mescaline, or other drugs—can hurt more than it helps. At a time when your emotions sometimes seem out of control, drugs can magnify those feelings. As painful as it may seem at times, learning to face conflicts and deal with pressures is part of growing into a healthy, happy adult. People who use drugs to escape unhappiness as teenagers may never find happiness as adults, even if they stop using drugs. In the next chapter, you will read about someone who thinks there are better ways than peyote to find happiness and spiritual satisfaction.

Questions for Discussion

1. Would you use peyote if it was offered to you? How would you know that what you were trying was really peyote?

2. Anyone who is not a member of the Native American Church who is caught with peyote risks penalties of up to fifteen years in prison, a fine of up to twenty-five thousand dollars, or both. Do you think it is fair that some people are penalized while others are not? Explain your answer.

3. There is concern that legalizing peyote use for Native Americans has opened the door for other people to claim they should have a right to use peyote or other drugs as part of their religion. How do you feel about this possibility?

6

A Personal Perspective on Peyote

You will not find Edward Pisachubbe at a peyote meeting this Saturday night—or any Saturday night. Pisachubbe, a Choctaw, was born in Oklahoma, where the peyote religion has its roots. He now lives in Texas, where peyote grows wild. Still he is against the use of peyote—in or out of church.[1]

First, hear what he has to say about the religious use of peyote:

> *I know one person made reference to there being more religion in a small box that has peyote in it than there is in the entire Southern Baptist Convention. Well, that's unfortunate, because the God I believe in is not contained in a box or 'religion' . . . My belief is in God's love, forgiveness, and helping others in need.*

Native American Church roadman Anthony Davis, a Pawnee, has been using peyote ceremonially for most of his life. Some Native Americans are against the use of peyote for any purpose.

Pisachubbe says he doesn't need a drug to increase his faith or enhance his religious feelings.

"I just don't believe that you can find God or spirituality in a bottle or a box or any physical substance that would change your emotions and alter your thinking," he says. By twisting reality, drugs may even make it harder, not easier, to find spiritual insights, he believes.

As a Baptist minister, Pisachubbe has counseled clients in drug and alcohol treatment programs, some of whom were Native American peyote users. "They were confused," says Pisachubbe. While the users felt they needed to give up all drugs and alcohol, they had trouble giving up peyote. They felt guilty about using it, but they also felt guilty about giving it up. Taught that peyote was part of their culture, these users felt they were betraying their heritage if they stopped practicing peyotism.

What about the claim that using peyote helps keep people from using alcohol and other drugs? Pisachubbe does not buy that. "I think it can have more of a triggering effect and an enhancing effect," he says. Anyone who says he or she uses peyote to stay sober doesn't understand the meaning of the word, Pisachubbe argues. To him, being sober means using no drugs at all, not even peyote. And that goes for outside of church, as well as in it.

"Why would I want to use something that's going to affect my digestive system and cause a lot of vomiting?" Pisachubbe asks. "I think we have enough problems that give us headaches without taking something to actually cause a headache and affect the blood pressure and cause cramps and fevers and disorientation."

Pisachubbe knows that peyote does not cause physical dependence, but he worries about the disturbing psychological reactions that can lead to physical harm. Like people who get high through meditation, exercise, art, or other activities, Pisachubbe has found ways to feel good without drugs. He volunteers at The Dallas Life Foundation, one of the largest homeless shelters in the country. "When I go down on holidays to help serve food, I look around at the people involved in that, and I see such a joy in the expressions on their faces. Not only that, but they talk about how good they feel," Pisachubbe says. That good feeling lasts much longer than the fleeting high from drugs.

"I can admit from personal experience that with a hangover, I never could honestly say, 'I feel great because I had a great time last night,'" says Pisachubbe. "I wouldn't go around telling people how good I feel and how happy I feel." But the high he gets from helping out at the homeless shelter is different.

I can counsel and work all day at other places and go down there in the evening and really be physically tired. But when I leave there, I'm emotionally uplifted, spiritually uplifted, as well as having some physical energy to walk away with. This is a 'spiritual high' I get from telling the clients there about going God's way. And I've had not one drop and not one pill of any kind.

Questions for Discussion

1. Name some positive activities that you could participate in to give you a natural "high."

2. Do you think it would be difficult to be a Native American who disagrees with peyote use? Why? Why not?

3. What would you do if you were a Native American who did not believe in ritual peyote use and you were being pressured by others to try it?

Chapter Notes

Chapter 1

1. Edward F. Anderson, *Peyote: The Divine Cactus* (Tucson, Ariz.: The University of Arizona Press, 1980), p. 8.

2. Richard Evans Schultes and Albert Hofmann, *Plants of the Gods: Their Sacred, Healing and Hallucinogenic Powers* (Rochester, Vt.: Healing Arts Press, 1992), p. 134.

3. Anderson, p. 12.

4. Personal interview with Stacy Schaefer, associate professor of anthropology, University of Texas-Pan American, April 1996.

5. Tom Mayers, "20 Years Visiting the Huichols," *Newsletter of the Multidisciplinary Association for Psychedelic Studies IV*, Spring 1993, pp. 29–31.

6. Stacy Schaefer, "The Crossing of the Souls: Peyote, Perception, and Meaning Among the Huichol Indians of Mexico," *People of the Peyote: Huichol Indian History, Religion, & Survival,* Stacy B. Schaefer and Peter T. Furst, eds. (Albuquerque, N.M.: University of New Mexico Press, 1996), p. 44.

7. Ibid., p. 35.

8. Ibid., pp. 35, 41.

9. Anderson, p. 2.

10. Omer C. Stewart, *Peyote Religion: A History* (Norman, Okla.: University of Oklahoma Press, 1987), p. 19.

11. Anderson, p. 7.

12. Schultes and Hofmann, p. 133.

13. Richard Evans Schultes, "An Overview of Hallucinogens in the Western Hemisphere," *Flesh of the Gods,* Peter T. Furst, ed. (Prospect Heights, Ill.: Waveland Press, Inc., 1990), p. 13.

14. Anderson, pp. 30–31.

15. Stewart, pp. 65–66.

16. Ibid., p. 78.

17. Ibid., p. 79.

18. Ibid., pp. 86–90.

19. Schultes, p. 13.

20. Omer C. Stewart, "Peyotism," Microsoft Encarta, 1994.

21. Omer C. Stewart, *Peyote Religion: A History* (Norman, Okla.: University of Oklahoma Press, 1987), p. 132.

22. Ibid., pp. 178–197.

23. Ibid., p. 98.

24. Ibid., p. 107.

25. Ibid., pp. 220–221.

26. Ibid., p. 169.

27. Claudia Glenn Dowling, "Woodstock," *Life 12*, August 1989, pp. 20–45.

28. Cited by David Solomon, ed., in *LSD: The Consciousness-Expanding Drug* (New York: G.P. Putnam's Son's, 1966), p. 63. Solomon cited in Edward M. Brecher and the Editors of Consumer Reports, *Licit and Illicit Drugs* (Boston: Little, Brown and Company, 1972), p. 339.

Chapter 2

1. Weston La Barre, *The Peyote Cult* (Hamden, Conn.: Archon Books, 1975), p. 11.

2. Ibid.

3. Richard Evans Schultes and Albert Hofmann, *Plants of the Gods: Their Sacred, Healing and Hallucinogenic Powers* (Rochester, Vt.: Healing Arts Press, 1992), p. 134.

4. Omer C. Stewart, *Peyote Religion: A History* (Norman, Okla.: University of Oklahoma Press, 1987), p. 19.

5. Peter T. Furst, "To Find Our Life: Peyote Among the Huichol Indians of Mexico," *Flesh of the Gods* (Prospect Heights, Ill.: Waveland Press, Inc., 1990), p. 180.

6. Schultes and Hofmann, p. 136.

7. Description of peyote pilgrimage was summarized from Schultes and Hofmann; Furst; personal interview with Stacy Schaefer, 1996; and Stacy Schaefer, "The Crossing of the Souls: Peyote, Perception and Meaning Among the Huichol Indians of Mexico," in *People of the Peyote: Huichol Indian History, Religion, & Survival*, Stacy B. Schaefer and Peter T. Furst, eds. (Albuquerque: University of New Mexico Press, 1996).

8. LaBarre, p. 57.

9. Texas Dept. of Public Safety, personal communication, 1996.

10. Louis Sahagun, "American Album: Peyote harvesters face supply-side problem," *Los Angeles Times*, June 13, 1994, p.5.

11. Texas Dept. of Public Safety, 1996.

12. Personal interview with Isabel Lopez, Oilton, Texas, peyote dealer, 1996.

13. Sahagun, p. 5.

14. Personal interview with Robert Billy Whitehorse, president, Native American Church of Navajoland, April 1996.

15. Jim W. Jones, "Using peyote: another way to reach God?" *Ft. Worth Star-Telegram,* March 3, 1996, p. 8.

16. Andrew Weil and Winifred Rosen, *From Chocolate to Morphine* (Boston: Houghton Mifflin Company, 1993), p. 107.

Chapter 3

1. William A. Emboden, Jr., *Narcotic Plants* (New York: Macmillan, 1972), p. 55.

2. Edward F. Anderson, *Peyote: The Divine Cactus* (Tucson, Ariz.: The University of Arizona Press, 1980), p. 79.

3. Christopher K. Koenigsberg, posting to Internet alt.drugs newsgroup, April 7, 1994.

4. Peter Stafford, *Psychedelics Encyclopedia,* Third Expanded Edition (Berkeley, Calif.: Ronin Publishing, Inc., 1992), p. 116.

5. Stacy Schaefer, "The Crossing of the Souls: Peyote, Perception, and Meaning Among the Huichol Indians of Mexico," in *People of the Peyote: Huichol Indian History, Religion, & Survival,* Stacy B. Schaefer and Peter T. Furst, eds. (Albuquerque, N.M.: University of New Mexico Press, 1996), p. 42.

6. Koenigsberg, Internet posting, April 7, 1994.

7. Emboden, p. 55.

8. Koenigsberg, Internet posting, April 7, 1994.

9. William Braden, *The Private Sea* (Chicago: Quadrangle Books, 1967), p. 232. Cited in Anderson, p. 71.

10. Erich Guttman and W.S. Maclay, "Mescalin and Depersonalization," *Journal of Neurology and Psychopathology 16,* January 1936, pp. 193–212.

11. R.C. Zaehner, Mysticism, *Sacred and Profane* (London: Oxford University Press, 1961), p. 211. Cited in Anderson, p. 69.

12. Ben Winton, "An Ancient Spirit: Peyote Guides Revealing Ritual," *The Phoenix Gazette,* September 8, 1990, p. A1.

13. Humphrey Osmond, "On Being Mad," in *Psychedelics,* Bernard Aaronson, and Humphrey Osmond, eds. (Garden City, N.Y.: Doubleday, 1970), pp. 26–27. Cited in Anderson, p. 73.

14. John Blofield, "A High Yogic Experience Achieved with Mescaline," *Psychedelic Review 7,* 1966, pp. 27–32. Cited in Anderson, p. 87.

15. Aldous Huxley, *The Doors of Perception and Heaven and Hell* (San Bernadino, Calif.: The Borgo Press, 1990), p. 55.

16. Zaehner, p. 209.

17. Richard Evans Schultes and Albert Hofmann, *Plants of the Gods: Their Sacred, Healing and Hallucinogenic Powers* (Rochester, Vt.: Healing Arts Press, 1992), p. 133.

18. Weston La Barre, *The Peyote Cult* (Hamden, Conn.: Archon Books, 1975), p.18.

19. Paul Radin, *Crashing Thunder: The Autobiography of a Winnebago Indian* (New York, 1926), pp. 198–199. Cited in La Barre, p. 18.

20. Stafford, p. 133.

21. Anderson, p. 93.

22. Andre Weil and Winifred Rosen, *From Chocolate to Morphine* (Boston: Houghton Mifflin Company, 1993), p. 107.

23. David L. Dorrance, Oscar Janiger, and Raymond L. Teplitz, "Effect of Peyote on Human Chromosomes," *JAMA 234* (1975), pp. 299-302.

24. P.C. Reynolds and E.J. Jindrich, "A Mescaline Associated Fatality," *Journal of Analytical Toxicology 9,* July–August 1985, pp. 183–184. Cited in "Mescaline: Its Effects and Composition," *PharmAlert* 19, 1990, p. 2.

25. Richard H. Schwartz, "Mescaline: A Survey," *American Family Physician* 37 (April 1988), pp. 122–124.

Chapter 4

1. Jerry Kammer, "The Soul of the People: Peyote Opens 'Access to God,'" *Arizona Republic,* September 19, 1993, p. NV1.

2. Entire section on Rex Harvey's peyote ceremony excerpted and paraphrased with permission from Phoenix Newspapers, Inc.

3. Omer C. Stewart, *Peyote Religion: A History* (Norman, Okla.:, University of Oklahoma Press, 1987), p. 224.

4. Omer C. Stewart, "Peyotism," *Microsoft Encarta,* 1994.

5. Personal interview with Robert Billy Whitehorse, April 1996.

6. Stewart, "Peyotism."

7. Ronald K. Bullis, "Swallowing the Scroll: Legal Implications of the Recent Supreme Court Peyote Cases," *Journal of Psychoactive Drugs* 22, July–September,1990, pp. 325–332.

8. "Must say no," *The Economist* 317, Oct. 6, 1990, p. 25.

9. Jim Jones, "Indians' Use of Peyote Once Again Under Seige" *Fort Worth Star-Telegram*, December 6, 1992, p. 1.

10. Nicholas Cozzi, "Ho Chunk Meeting." Council on Spiritual Practices Home Page, World Wide Web, November 1994.

11. Jones, p.1.

12. Richard Evans Schultes and Albert Hofmann, *Plants of the Gods: Their Sacred, Healing and Hallucinogenic Powers* (Rochester, Vt.: Healing Arts Press, 1992), p.143.

13. Main sources for description of peyote ceremony were Cozzi, 1994, and Edward F. Anderson, *Peyote: The Divine Cactus* (Tucson, Ariz: The University Press, 1980).

14. Personal interview with Robert Billy Whitehorse, 1996.

15. Anderson, p. 59.

16. Omer C. Stewart, *Peyote Religion: A History* (Norman, Okla.: University of Oklahoma Press, 1987), p. 157.

17. Ibid. p. 118.

18. Ibid., p. 193.

19. Robert L. Bergman, MD, "Navajo Peyote Use: Its Apparent Safety," *American Journal of Psychiatry 128,* December 1971, pp. 695–699.

20. Reuben A. Snake, Jr., September 29, 1990, Washington, D.C. Speech presented during a prayer day organized by Native American Church leaders; posted to Internet, February 16, 1995, by Eric E. Sterling, president of The Criminal Justice Policy Foundation.

21. Personal interview with Robert Billy Whitehorse, April 1996.

22. Anderson, p. 168.

23. "Peyote Use Ruled Legal in Indian Rite," *San Francisco Chronicle,* August 25, 1964, pp.1, 11. Cited in Anderson, p. 168.

24. Debbie Howlett, "High Court to Rule on Religious Use of Peyote," *USA Today,* November 6, 1989, p. 56.

25. Rob Boston, "Peyote Impasse," *Church & State 5*, February 1990, pp. 8–12.

26. Michael McConnell, "Freedom From Religion?" *American Enterprise 4*, January/February, 1993, pp. 34–43.

Chapter 5

1. Weston La Barre, *The Peyote Cult* (Hamden, Conn.: Archon Books, 1975), p. 15.

2. Edward F. Anderson, *Peyote: The Divine Cactus* (Tucson, Ariz.: The University of Arizona Press, 1980), pp. 93–94.

3. Paula Kurtzweil, "Medical Possibilities For Psychedelic Drugs," *FDA Consumer 29*, September 1995, pp. 25–28.

4. Gilda Berger, Addiction: Its Causes, Problems, and Treatments (New York: Franklin Watts, 1982), p. 41. Cited in "Mescaline: Its Effects and Composition," *PharmAlert 19*, 1990, p. 1.

5. Anderson, p. 140.

6. Jerry Mandel and Harvey W. Feldman, "The Social History of Teenage Drug Use," in *Teen Drug Use,* George Beschner and Alfred S. Friedman, eds. (Lexington, Mass.: Lexington Books, 1986), pp. 26–27.

7. National Institute on Drug Abuse, "National Household Survey on Drug Abuse: Trends in Substance Abuse, 1979–1994," U.S. Department of Health and Human Services: Washington, D.C., 1995.

8. C.L. Renfroe and T.A. Messinger, "Street drug analysis: an eleven year perspective on illicit drug alteration." *Semin. Adoles. Med. 1,* 1985, pp. 247-257. Cited in Schwartz, 1988.

9. Peter Stafford, *Psychedelics Encyclopedia,* Third Expanded Edition (Berkeley, Calif.: Ronin Publishing, Inc., 1992), p. 119.

10. National Institute on Drug Abuse, "National Household Survey on Drug Abuse: Discussion of Results," U.S. Department of Health and Human Services: Washington, D.C., 1995.

11. Andrew Weil and Winifred Rosen, *From Chocolate to Morphine* (Boston: Houghton Mifflin Company, 1993), p. 175.

Chapter 6

1. Chapter based on personal interview with Edward Pisachubbe, April 10, 1996.

Where to Write

If you or someone you know has a drug problem, you do not have to feel hopeless. There are plenty of places to find help. School counselors, ministers, and other trusted adults can guide you to treatment programs. You can also check the Yellow Pages of your local telephone directory, under the heading, "Drug Abuse and Addiction—Information and Treatment." There, you will find phone numbers for treatment programs, some of which may have twenty-four-hour help lines. In some communities, you'll also find phone numbers you can call to hear recorded messages on such topics as "Signs of Drug Abuse." Listed below are national help lines, organizations, and World Wide Web sites that can provide information on drug abuse and treatment.

Hot Lines

Center for Substance Abuse Treatment
National Drug and Alcohol Treatment Referral Service
(800) 662-4357
Provides information referrals to treatment programs and support organizations. Twenty-four-hour service.

National Council on Alcoholism and Drug Dependence Hopeline
(800) 622-2255
Twenty-four-hour service that refers callers to local affiliate offices of the National Council on Alcoholism and Drug Dependence. Callers can also leave their names and addresses to receive written information about alcohol and other drug abuse (most information available is on alcoholism). Touch tone phone is required.

Organizations and Agencies

American Council for Drug Education
164 West 74th Street
New York, NY 10023
(800) 488-3784

"Just Say No" International
2101 Webster St.
Suite 1300
Oakland, CA 94612
(800) 258-2766
Does not provide treatment referrals or printed materials on specific drugs, but has information on the Youth Power program, which empowers young people to live healthy, productive, drug-free lives.

National Clearinghouse for Alcohol and Drug Information
PO Box 2345
Rockville, MD 20847-2345
(800) 729-6686

World Wide Web Sites

Canadian Centre on Substance Abuse
<http://www.ccsa.ca/>
Nonprofit organization dedicated to reducing the harmful effects of alcohol, tobacco, and other drug use. Databases on Canadian substance abuse resources, treatment services and organizations. Answers information requests.

National Clearinghouse for Alcohol and Drug Information (NCADI)
<http://www.health.org/>
One of the world's largest resources for information on alcohol and other drugs. Offers fact sheets, videos, posters, and bibliographies. Databases: Information on Drugs & Alcohol (IDA), Prevline (Prevention On-line), Citizen's guides, and Substance Abuse Information Database (SAID).

National Institute on Drug Abuse (NIDA)
<http://www.nida.nih.gov>
Home page has information on NIDA publications, videos, and fact sheets.

Partnership for a Drug Free Community

<http://fly.HiWAAY.net/~partner/>

Nonprofit organization concerned with preventing alcohol and drug abuse among young people. Provides information on community sevices; local, national, and international resources.

Web of Addictions

<http://www.well.com/www/woa>

Aims to provide accurate information about alcohol and other drugs to teachers, students, and the public.

Glossary

addiction—An overwhelming urge or physical need to use a drug repeatedly. Signs of addiction include cravings, the need to increase doses over time to get the same effect, and the presence of withdrawal symptoms. Withdrawal symptoms are symptoms that appear when a person stops taking the drug and disappear when the person starts taking the drug again.

alkaloid—A nitrogen-containing compound produced by plants. Many alkaloids have mind-altering effects. Some are poisonous and some have medicinal uses.

anthropologist—A scientist who studies the physical attributes, origins, environment, social relationships, and cultures of human beings.

auditory hallucinations—Hearing sounds that are not really there.

bad trip—An unpleasant experience while under the influence of a drug, especially a hallucinogen. Panic, depression, and paranoia may occur during a bad trip.

bona fide—Genuine.

botanist—A scientist who studies plants and plant life.

button—The dried top of a peyote cactus plant.

chromosome—A thread-shaped structure, made up of DNA and protein, found in the nucleus of plant and animal cells. Genes, which carry genetic instructions that are essential to life, are short lengths of chromosomes.

coma—A deep, long-lasting period of unconsciousness.

cross-tolerance—Tolerance to a drug that develops after using another, similar drug.

depersonalization—Feeling that the mind and body are not connected.

Ghost Dance—A religion that attracted thousands of Native Americans in the 1890s. It combined traditional Native American dance ceremonies with Christian teachings.

111

hallucination—A vision of something that is not really there.

hallucinogens—Drugs that alter perception and mood. Examples are LSD, peyote, and mescaline.

high—An altered state of consciousness in which a person has a feeling of happiness, well-being, and high energy.

hippies—People who rejected the established rules of society during the 1960s and 1970s and were known for dressing unconventionally and using hallucinogenic drugs.

kiva—A round ceremonial building that is partly underground.

mescaline—The main active ingredient of peyote. Mescaline is an alkaloid.

methoxyamphetamines—Drugs that are combinations of mescaline and amphetamines. MDMA, also known as Ecstasy, is an example.

missionaries—People sent by a church to spread its faith or carry out humanitarian acts.

neurotransmitter—A chemical released by nerve cells. It carries nerve impulses across gaps in the nervous system.

norepinephrine—A neurotransmitter that affects heart rate, blood pressure, body temperature, and other body functions.

paranoia—An unfounded suspicion that other people are plotting against a person or doing things behind his or her back.

PCP—Phencyclidine, also known as angel dust. A hallucinogenic drug that alters the ability to think clearly and makes people act unpredictably—sometimes violently. PCP is psychologically addictive, and it can cause convulsions or coma.

peyotero—A person who gathers peyote. In the United States peyoteros are licensed to sell peyote to Native Americans.

peyote road—The path of righteous living that a peyotist tries to follow throughout life.

peyotism—The religious use of peyote.

peyotist—A person who practices peyotism.

physical dependence—A condition in which a drug user needs the drug to function normally and suffers withdrawal symptoms if he or she stops taking the drug.

pilgrimage—A journey to a sacred place.

polydrug use—Using more than one drug at once.

pseudohallucination—A false hallucination; a distortion of what is perceived.

psychedelics—Another term for hallucinogens.

psychological dependence—A condition in which a drug user craves a drug to feel good.

reservations—Land set aside specifically for Native Americans.

roadman—The leader of a Native American peyote ceremony.

Schedule I drug—Any drug considered to have a high potential for abuse, present an unacceptable safety risk, and have no accepted medical use.

schizophrenia—A form of mental illness that affects thought and perception.

shaman—A traditional priest who contacts spirits to learn hidden truths or cure the sick.

shrine—A place for prayer.

strychnine—A kind of poison.

synthesize—Create a chemical compound in a laboratory by combining simpler ingredients.

tolerance—A decrease in sensitivity to a drug. When a user develops tolerance to a drug, he or she must keep increasing its dosage to get the same effect.

trip—An experience under the influence of a drug, especially a hallucinogen.

tuberculosis—A highly contagious disease of the lungs.

underground chemist—A chemist who manufactures drugs illegally to sell on the street.

Further Reading

Anderson, Edward F. *Peyote:The Divine Cactus.* Tucson, Ariz.: The University of Arizona Press, 1980.

Charles, Sharon Ashenbrenner, and Sari Feldman. *Drugs: A Multimedia Sourcebook for Young Adults.* New York: Neal Schumann, 1980.

Emboden, William. *Narcotic Plants.* New York: Macmillan, 1979.

Green, Bernard. *Getting Over Getting High: How to Overcome Dependency on Cocaine, Caffeine, Hallucinogens, Marijuana, Speed, and Other Stimulants the Natural and Permanent Way.* New York: Quill, 1985.

Hyde, Margaret O., editor. *Mind Drugs.* New York: McGraw-Hill, 1974.

Richardson, P. Mick. *Flowering Plants: Magic in Bloom.* New York: Chelsea House Publishers, 1986.

Rosenfeld, Edward. *The Book of Highs: 250 Methods for Altering Your Consciousness Without Drugs.* New York: Quadrangle/New York Times Book Co., 1973.

Schultes, Richard Evans. *Hallucinogenic Plants.* New York: Golden Press, 1976.

Stewart, Omer C., *Peyote Religion: A History.* Norman, Okla.: University of Oklahoma Press, 1987.

Weil, Andrew, and Winifred Rosen. *From Chocolate to Morphine: Everything You Need to Know About Mind-Altering Drugs.* Boston: Houghton Mifflin Company, 1993.

Internet Addresses

The World Wide Web has greatly enhanced access to reputable and authoritative information on Peyote. Information is current, often available without a trip to a library, and relatively easy to find. Most government agencies and professional organizations now make many of their resources available electronically on the web. Previously these publications were typically available only in print and only by request or from a library.

On the other hand, with more than one billion indexable web sites to choose from, it is difficult to find exactly what you want. A search engine may retrieve thousands of sites. How do you find the ones you need? Even worse, there is a lot of inaccurate, confusing, and even strange information available on the web. Anyone can "publish" anything on the web! There are no requirements that the information be verified or reviewed before it is made available. Web sites may not be stable and can disappear at any time.

This chapter identifies and annotates some of the best, most authoritative, and stable sites on the web which deal with Peyote.

Internet Addresses researched by: Greg Byerly and Carolyn S. Brodie are Associate Professors in the School of Library and Information Science, Kent State University and write a monthly Internet column titled COMPUTER CACHE for *School Library Media Activities Monthly.*

WEB SITES WITH INFORMATION ON PEYOTE

The American Indian Religious Freedom Act of 1978

<http://www.usbr.gov/laws/airfa.html>

Read a brief summary of the American Indian Religious Freedom Act of 1978 on this site from the United States Bureau of Reclamation. A link is also provided to the actual federal legislation.

Botany of Peyote

<http://www.druglibrary.org/schaffer/lsd/pbotany.htm>

Provides a detailed botanical history of peyote. Differentiates between various common names for peyote and identifies plants which are commonly confused with peyote. This is an electronic version of a chapter in Edward F. Anderson's book, *The Divine Cactus* (The University of Arizona Press, 1980) on "Peyote."

Bureau of Indian Affairs

<http://www.doi.gov/bureau-indian-affairs.html>

Given the close association of peyote with Native Americans and the on-going fight to make the ceremonial use of peyote legal, this official government site from the U.S. Bureau of Indian Affairs can be consulted to find current information on the various issues related to Native Americans, including the use of peyote.

Cactus

<http://microscopy.fsu.edu/primer/techniques/fluorescence/gallery/cactus.html>

Not a lot of information, but this is the only site where you can find a full-color photomicrograph (photographs taken through a microscope) of a cactus and read about the peyote cactus (genus *Lophophora*).

A Field Full of Buttons

<http://www.peyote.com/peyote/index.html>

Read an article published in *The Economist* (April 3, 1999) which describes "America's most unusual crop: peyote, a small, mind-altering cactus used for 10,000 years as an Indian religious sacrament." Describes the historical use of peyote, legal cultivation efforts, and how increased use has decreased the supply of peyote.

The Huichol of Mexico:
Their Culture, Symbolism and Art

<http://mexconnect.com/mex_/huichol/huicholindex.html>

This contemporary site on the Huichol of Mexico provides great insight into the ceremonial use of peyote. Relevant sections include: The Huichol, the People; Huichol Indians, Their Art & Symbols; Huichol Shamanic Art; and Comprehending Shamanism.

Imaging and Imagining the Ghost Dance

<http://php.indiana.edu/~tkavanag/visual5.html>

A fascinating series of paintings and actual photographs of the Ghost Dance of 1890. The images come from a 1896 report by James Mooney to the Smithsonian Institution Bureau of American Ethnology. Besides illustrations of the ceremony, portraits of Sitting Bull the Hunkpapa and scenes of Wounded Knee are included. There are eight illustrations of the Dance in progress.

The Mescal Bean And The Unrelated Peyote Cactus

<http://daphne.palomar.edu/wayne/peyote.htm#loco6b.gif>

Provides color photographs of the peyote cactus (*Lophophora williamsii*), the desert shrub called mescal bean (*Sophora secundiflora*), and the Pacific coastal psilocybin mushroom (*Psilocybe cyanescens*). Notes the potent hallucinogenic power of these plants.

Peyote
<http://www.erowid.org/plants/peyote/peyote.shtml>

While this site promotes the use of peyote as a "potential tool for spiritual and personal growth," the site is a great resource for peyote information. Sections include: Peyote Legal Status, The Peyote Religion, Native/Non-Native Use, Peyote Timeline, Shamanism and Peyote Use Among the Apaches, Botany of Peyote (classification information), and Peyote and other Psychoactive Cacti.

Peyote
<http://www.drugabuse.com/drugs/peyote/>

This site from DrugAbuse.com provides basic factual information about peyote in the following categories: description, background, usage, effects, dependency, and treatment.

Peyote & Mescaline
<http://www.usdoj.gov/dea/concern/abuse/chap5/peyote.htm>

A part of the Drugs of Abuse web site presented by the U.S. Department of Justice Drug Enforcement Administration (DEA), this site briefly describes peyote and mescaline. Click on Drugs of Abuse Hallucinogens Chapter to access additional information on other types of hallucinogens.

The Peyote Foundation
<http://www.peyote.net/>

This Peyote Foundation web site includes sections on Peyote as an Inspirational Medicine, Traditional Rehabilitative Therapy, Peyote's ancient history of Religious use, and Natural Populations of Peyote in Decline. There are many links to other peyote religion sites. Emphasis is on the use of peyote in Native American religion.

The Peyote Way Church
<http://www.peyoteway.org/>

This is the official web site of the Peyote Way Church, "A non-denominational All Race Peyotist Religion." While the beliefs expressed can be controversial, there is a lengthy chronology of "significant events at the Peyote Way Church since 1977" which outlines efforts to legalize the use of peyote in the United States. The beliefs of the Peyote Way Church are succinctly, if not dubiously, stated as "The Religious Use of Peyote Has Never Harmed Anyone."

Psilocybin and Mescaline
<http://www.chm.bris.ac.uk/motm/psilocybin/psilocybinh.htm>
Chemical formulae for psilocybin and mescaline are diagramed and color pictures are provided of both "magic mushrooms" and the peyote cactus. Briefly discusses the possible relationship between hallucinogenic drugs and schizophrenia.

Quanah Parker
<http://www.stainblue.com/quanahparker.html>
Learn about the life of Quanah Parker, a Commanche chief who was "influential in the spread of Christian peyotism among the Plains Indians." This brief biographical sketch also describes the "peyote experience."

The Tracks of the Little Deer
<http://peyote.org/>
Provides a detailed history of the use of peyote by Native Americans and describes various peyote ceremonies. Notes that peyote is used as a religious sacrament by more than forty American Indian tribes in the United States and Canada. This material is reproduced from *Plants of the Gods: Their Sacred, Healing and Hallucinogenic Powers* by Richard Evans Schultes and Albert Hoffman (Healing Arts Press, 1992).

GENERAL DRUG SITES WITH INFORMATION ON PEYOTE

American Council for Drug Education
<http://www.acde.org/>
The American Council for Drug Education (ACDE) is "a substance abuse prevention and education agency that develops

programs and materials based on the most current scientific research on drug use and its impact on society." The site offers extensive materials for youth, college students, parents, health professionals, educators, and employees. The following substances are covered by the site: Alcohol, Cocaine/Crack, Heroin, Inhalants, Marijuana, Methamphetamine, and Tobacco. ACDE is associated with Phoenix House, a nationally recognized leader in the treatment of substance abuse (http://www.phoenixhouse.org/).

D.A.R.E.
<http://DARE.com/>

This is the official site of D.A.R.E. (Drug Abuse Resistance Education). In addition to providing news about the D.A.R.E. organization, this site offers D.A.R.E. Kids, an interactive and fun site for kids with its own Clubhouse.

Get It Straight: The Facts About Drugs
<http://www.usdoj.gov/dea/pubs/straight/cover.htm>

This site includes the full-text of *Get it Straight! The Facts about Drugs*, published by the U.S. Department of Justice's Drug Enforcement Administration. It is designed to help teenagers "realize that using drugs is not the way to go. The book will also be helpful as a research tool for your school assignments, as something fun to read, and also as something to share with your friends." Each section deals with a specific category of drugs. Questionnaires, word searches, and other fun exercises are included in this hypothetical class assignment for teenagers.

Moyers on Addiction
<http://www.pbs.org/wnet/closetohome/home.html>

Companion to the five-part 1998 PBS television series, Moyers on Addiction: Close to Home. Host Bill Moyers looked at the science, treatment, prevention, and politics of drug addiction in the United States. This site continues to provide guides for each of the topics covered in the five episodes. In addition to providing background information and facts about addiction, in each case the experience of addiction is vividly described by someone who has experienced it. Animated graphics are used to demonstrate the effects of drugs on the brain and body.

Narcotics and Substance Abuse

<http://usinfo.state.gov/topical/global/drugs/>

Information from the U.S. Department of State concerning drug trafficking and substance abuse. Key documents in U.S. drug policy are available and links are provided to the principal federal agencies which deal with drugs in the United States. This is a good source for up-to-date statistics and other information about drug use, drugs and crime, and prevention and treatment.

Narcotics Anonymous

<http://www.wsoinc.com/>

Starting in 1947 as an outgrowth of Alcoholics Anonymous, Narcotics Anonymous, this site primarily deals with organizational news and history. However, it does provide access to numerous Public Information Guides and other information about narcotic addiction.

National Center on Addiction and Substance Abuse at Columbia University

<http://www.casacolumbia.org/>

Known as the Center for Addiction and Substance Abuse (CASA), this organization presents a wide variety of information on the impact and cost, both to individuals and communities, of drug use and abuse. Two sections of the site are especially useful. Resources and Links provides a wide-ranging lists of links to drug-related web sites in categories such as Federal Resources, Grant Making and Funding Resources, Kids and Teens Resources, Nonprofit Resources, Treatment and Recovery Resources, and Web Search Resources.

National Clearinghouse for Alcohol and Drug Information (NCADI)
PREVLINE: Prevention Online

<http://www.health.org/>

PREVLINE, Prevention Online, is the web site for the National Clearinghouse for Alcohol and Drug Information (NCADI). NCADI is a service of the Center for Substance Abuse Prevention, which is under the Substance Abuse and Mental Health Services Administration (SAMHSA). The site includes Research Briefs, Workplace Issues, Resources & Referrals, Related Links, Alcohol & Drug Facts, Funding/Grants, Online Forums, and a Kids Area.

Girl Power!

<http://www.girlpower.gov/index.htm>

Girl Power! is a national public education campaign sponsored by the U.S. Department of the Health and Human Services to "help encourage and motivate 9- to 14- year-old girls to make the most of their lives." There are separate sections for girls and parents, as well as Research and News About Girls. While this fun site is about all aspects of girls' health, it includes information about the harmful effects of drugs on young women.

For Kids Only

<http://www.health.org/features/kidsarea/INDEX.htm>

This site NCADI is "For Kids Only." Visually appealing and lots of fun, games and other activities are used to address such issues as "Be Smart, Don't Start" and "Internet Safety." Answers are also suggested for questions such as "How Can I Say No?" and "How Can I Help Someone?" Great for elementary and middle school students. This site is also available in Spanish.

National Institute on Drug Abuse
<http://www.nida.nih.gov/>

The National Institute on Drug Abuse (NIDA) is an agency within the U.S. Department of Health and Human Services. This site includes research findings, news releases, publications, legislation information, and links to other NIDA resources. Like NCADI, NIDA is an excellent source for accurate and informative materials about all aspects of drug use and abuse.

Commonly Abused Drugs: Street Names for Drugs of Abuse
<http://www.nida.nih.gov/DrugsofAbuse.html>

Similar to Information on Common Drugs of Abuse, this web page provides a chart which lists street names, medical uses, delivery systems, and other information for various Stimulants, Hallucinogens, Opioids and Morphine Derivatives, and Depressants.

Office of National Drug Control Policy
<http://www.whitehousedrugpolicy.gov/>

The Office of National Drug Control Policy (ONDCP) is a great source for information on a variety of drug-related topics. It sponsors and supports a wide variety of other web sites.

Drugs Facts and Stats
<http://www.whitehousedrugpolicy.gov/drugfact/>

A great source for statistics and facts about drug use and abuse in the United States. The Facts and Figures section provides direct access by drug name to an overview of the problem with the specific drug and current statistics on its prevalence.

National Youth Anti-Drug Media Campaign
<http://www.mediacampaign.org/mg/index.html>

The Media Gallery of the National Youth Anti-Drug Campaign provides direct access to current promotional efforts using television, print, radio, and banner ads.

FreeVibe

<http://www.freevibe.com/>

Freevibe was developed by the White House Office of National Drug Control Policy in collaboration with the Center for Substance Abuse Prevention (CSAP) and other partners. The site is visually appealing and designed to attract youths 11-14.

Partnership for a Drug Free America

<http://www.drugfreeamerica.org/>

The Drug-Free Resource Net of the Partnership for a Drug-Free America (PDFA) is an excellent source for fairly detailed information about many different drugs, including Marijuana, Inhalants, LSD, PCP, Peyote, Cocaine/Crack, Designer Drugs, Steroids, Tobacco, Alcohol, and Heroin. You can click on "What the drugs look like" to find pictures of drugs and you can go to "Paraphernalia" to find pictures of drug paraphernalia.

Planet Know

<http://www.planet-know.net/first.htm>

Planet Know, a Planet Free of Drugs, is a site designed to attract teenagers—it's animated, colorful, and creatively designed. Teens can dial "411" and take a quiz about Marijuana, Inhalants, Heroin, Hallucinogens, and Cocaine. This site needs to be explored to uncover all of its attractions.

Index